POWER
in the BLOOD

POWER in the BLOOD

LAND, MEMORY, and a SOUTHERN FAMILY

JOHN BENTLEY MAYS

With photographs by Richard Rhodes

HarperCollins*Publishers*

HarperCollins books may be purchased for educational, business, or sales promotional use. For information please write: Special Markets Department, HarperCollins Publishers, Inc., 10 East 53rd Street, New York, NY 10022.

FIRST EDITION

Designed by Alma Hochhauser Orenstein

Photographs copyright © by Richard Rhodes

Library of Congress Cataloging-in-Publication Data

Mays, John Bentley.
    Power in the blood : land, memory, and a southern family / John Bentley Mays.
        p.   cm.
    ISBN 0-06-018269-5
    1. Mays, John Bentley—Journeys—Southern States. 2. Mays, John Bentley—Childhood and youth. 3. Greenwood (N.C.)—Biography. 4. Southern States—History. 5. Southern States—Social life and customs. 6. May family.   I. Title.
F624.G84M39   1997
975'.04'092—dc21
[B]   97-15040

97 98 99 00 01 ❖/RRD 10 9 8 7 6 5 4 3 2 1

To Margaret,
for twenty-six years

Contents

About This Book

POWER IN THE BLOOD IS A MEMOIR OF MY FAMILY DURING THE FIRST FOUR centuries of our tenure on Southern ground, a recollection of the places we have dwelt and worked, and the mental worlds we have inhabited. It is also the record of my inner struggle to resolve, or at least to understand, the conflict between my Southern heritage and the life I now live, outside the South.

It was not a struggle I invited, nor one that I welcomed. Thus the name of this book, which comes from an old gospel song about the power in Jesus' blood, drawing men and women from alienation into the difficult path to the reconciling Cross. I intend no impiety by this title: for my answering of the call of Christ's blood long ago was what first taught me to recognize the powers in ancestral blood to teach and warn, lead and heal.

I set foot upon this second crimson road to personal identity as a stranger, and a stranger I have remained throughout the walking of it. This must be said; for I knew from the outset that, were this book to speak any truth at all, I would have to acknowledge continually my own *far* view, and my displacements into Modernity that lie behind the quest chronicled here. Hence, the shaping of the work as a critical dialogue between the present I inhabit and the past from which I come.

Hence, also, the *second* text interleaved with my own: the portfolio of images by the Canadian photographer Richard Rhodes, who went to the dwelling places of my ancestors and kin at my request, to record his encounters, as stranger and distanced witness, with

these Southern terrains. The pictures he brought back are not illus-
trations, or commentaries on what I have written, but rather the
offering of another way to see the Southern land, other windows
opening toward the terrain of Southern imagination I have traversed, and described in this book.

JOHN BENTLEY MAYS
Toronto, 1997

THE SECRET HOARD

Screened porch, Greenwood

The oldest of the old
follows us in our thinking,
yet ever comes forward to meet us.
                                    —MARTIN HEIDEGGER

THOUGH I DID NOT KNOW IT AT THE TIME, THE MAKING OF THIS book began on a spring morning in 1990, when Aunt Vandalia died in the Louisiana hilltop village of Greenwood. Apart from servants holding vigil elsewhere in the house as the old lady's rasping breath slowed in the dark that morning, then stopped, she was alone. No friends were there, and no children, for she had borne none. Her near blood kin had died before her, all but my sister and me, anyway—and the two of us were far away, in the places we'd gone after we left the South.

Vandalia went down to silence with the gradual physical quieting that enables the rest of us to bear, and even welcome, the dying of the old. Her body had begun to corrode and fade after her husband's death the spring before; he took with him into the town cemetery's upcountry clay the last reason she could find not to die.

Throughout his decline, she had tended Uncle Alvin—the handsome manager of her father's lands and cotton gins who'd stolen the heart of the boss's daughter—with fanatical zeal, refusing him the permission to die called for by courtesy and by plain common sense. After each day of exasperating her servants, and exhausting both Uncle Alvin and herself with desperate ministrations, she would collapse in a chair behind her cluttered oak secretary and write up the dosages—when administered and how and in what quantity—and note each barely microscopic change in his mood or appearance. On these strange pages, eventually piled into a niche in her oak desk, she also scribbled reminders to herself to telephone one or another of the quacks who preyed remorselessly upon her, taking her dollars in return for dire or ambiguous warnings, uplifting fantasies of cure, and prescriptions for yet more expensive nostrums, courses of treatment, and busy things she could do at home for her ward. Ailing for no other reason than great old age, Uncle Alvin endured these invasions impatiently, until he could endure them no longer. Whereupon he died, and left nothing for Aunt Vandalia to do other than begin her own dying.

Had I not quickly flown back home to Toronto after we buried Uncle Alvin the year before, I might have noted the advent of death in Aunt Vandalia's life—the onset of those slowings of animal motions, and the tremor of hands lightly tick-tocking as she passed through shadowy rooms in which she had played as a girl and lived almost sixty years as a married woman. I might have registered the morbid trembling a couple of days after Uncle Alvin's death, when she almost let slip her Bible. I lunged to catch the old book before it hit the floor and shattered. The leather spine was raw, dry, and crackled, the stitchery slack and frayed, the pages loose from years of being thumbed through for consolation against the vicissitudes of living and the enigma of dying. But if I noticed this or any other new uncertainty in her step or grasp, I put it out of my mind. Our young widows die young, I've heard people in my family say, or they marry some no-count somebody, which is like dying, only slower. But our old widows—Lord, they do live forever!

Never imagining Aunt Vandalia would not live forever, I neglected visits to the South, and only occasionally spoke to my kinswoman by telephone. There would always be time, I thought, for asking questions never asked about my parents and kin, for settling old unresolved quarrels with her over family business. Too, my job as art critic for a metropolitan daily newspaper, my life with wife and daughter, among friends, and within a great northern city beyond America, left little room in my crowded mind for thoughts of my elderly aunt, who seemed looked-after well enough. Then she died, and, on going back, I remembered something I had noticed at the time of Alvin's death, and filed away into forgetfulness. It had to do with skin.

Her dying had begun in earnest, it seemed to me, with a clouding of the pale, translucent skin prized by Southern ladies of her era, skin the South's subtropic blaze had never been allowed to shine full and hot upon. I remember her distress over young women coming of age in the 1950s, tanning their hides under the pitiless Southern sun. Vandalia believed they were recklessly discarding their most wonderful physical gift and, with it, the privilege of Southern womanhood itself—all in exchange for the barbarism of informality, half-nakedness, an ugly bronzed complexion. Skin aglow like a marble column at dusk by the Mediterranean, lucidly white yet tinted with the most delicate rose and fawn ... Did these females not understand that such was the priceless endowment of every respectable white Southern woman, however plain, however beautiful? The guarantee of status in the village matriarchy? Could they not see that perfect skin is *womanhood's sweetest allure*, the *radiance of true nobility* as proclaimed in the beauty and fashion magazines from the 1920s she'd saved and heaped in the attic? The only additional punishments these "new" women could inflict on themselves, thus irreversibly ruining their "prospects," would be smoking and drinking. And, to her dismay, they were starting to do that also.

Aunt Vandalia was the last woman I have ever known whose reverence for clear complexion was ideological, with scarcely a trace of cosmetic or hygienic agenda. According to the doctrine handed down through generations of Southern women, skin and character are inseparable, and, indeed, almost identical. To be worthy of her class, station, and sex, hence a candidate for marriage and social elevation, presupposed white skin. Long after her mother and the other local matriarch-guardians were dead, and the once-isolated farming town had been engulfed by suburbia spilling from the nearby metropolis of Shreveport—and a very long time after anybody cared—Vandalia cared deeply about skin. There was danger to honor in the South's hard summer sunshine—temptations to luxury, laziness, sensuality—and Aunt Vandalia's concern with her skin was concern for her honor. To become coarsened by the sun could lead to certain inner doubts about character—doubts that might then weaken one's resolve to resist wantonness and shame. Hence, Aunt Vandalia kept her skin and soul safe from solar turpitude, even when overseeing the garden help among her sun-thirsty roses. I recall the sight of her in early middle age, rambling along the bright paths between rosebushes and flower beds, her plunger-operated poison sprayer at the ready, swathed in veils of gauze, bottled up in tall collar and long sleeves, shadowed under a straw hat broad as our Christmas turkey platter and knotted securely under her chin.

Such concerns, I was reminded, were hardly limited to the women in my family. At an age so early I do not remember it, I learned to gauge, in minute units, one's depravity or respectability by noting the texture and tint of skin. And many years after leaving the South—and trying to put behind me all the snobbery and subtle racism involved—I still cannot use the word *redneck* in the manner Yankees do, as a vague synonym for all Southerners who aren't planters, blacks, belles, or authors. It remains for me a word charged with old exactitudes, denoting immediately damaged character made manifest in damaged skin, and with urgencies similar to those that haunted Aunt Vandalia's last year, prompting her to withdraw from the world into death's antechamber immediately upon the onset of what she imagined to be the clouding of her complexion. In this unseen realm, she was visited by dejection, intensified by the dying of elderly friends and her gradual fall under the total administration of servants. That end, everyone, everywhere, who lives to be very old must face. But the powers of skin theory to isolate and intimidate, to regulate one's passage through life, may seem exotic to anyone who comes upon this book without knowledge of Southern peculiarities—though acquaintance with the strictly hierarchical body culture of contemporary Beverly Hills, of all American places most like Dixie in this regard, may be helpful for understanding how impressive such powers can be.

When the nurse telephoned me in Toronto the morning after my aunt's death, I asked what she recalled hearing Miss Vannie say last, and she replied it had to do with not being ready to die. *Who is?* I almost replied, but did not. I knew the ground of her secret dread, which, on being reminded of it again, struck me as strange and sad as her lifelong bother about skin. Uncle Alvin, her husband of sixty years, had been married before, and divorced, thereby making of her marriage, at least in her moral imagination, *possibly* a prolonged adultery worthy of everlasting punishment. She was never sure. The

leaders of her Methodist church would perhaps not have openly condoned such a match, but neither would they have stopped it. Perhaps
both she and Uncle Alvin would have been happier had the church
done so, sending the couple off to find certifiably blameless partners.
As it was, throughout all those decades of married life, she believed
what she did as a young woman *might have been* a sin worthy of eternal retribution, and so had apparently died fearful and unprepared.

This news from the South struck me as worrisome, though not
because I was concerned about the direction Aunt Vandalia's soul
had sped upon release from its carnal wrapper. What bothered me
was the abrupt reinvasion of my mind that morning by certain
thoughts of Southern paths of being, belief, and death I'd given little
mind to in years. Indeed, distance from the obsessions and introspec-
tion shadowing these essential paths—the freedom to live as an
urban, thinking, Christian believer, unembarrassed by the oddity
stirring behind the smiling face of Southern popular religion—were
among the allures that, by the early 1960s, when I was ready for
graduate school, had me spending more time outside the region than
in it, and would eventually draw me out of the South altogether.
Back in those days, when I was trying to be *very* Modern, I would
have pronounced Aunt Vandalia's unhealing preoccupation with the
validity of her marriage, had I known of it, merely absurd.

But by the night of Vandalia's death, I had lived long enough, and
muddled through enough moral confusions, to see this early arro-
gance severely curtailed. That's not to say my attempts in the 1960s
to become Modern had been anything other than serious, nor my
haughtiness honestly earned. I wanted to unmoor myself from the
rural South of my upbringing, particularly the thicket of taboo and
restriction hedging in all hierarchical societies rooted in the land, in
the cultivation and culture of it, and I went about this project of self-
transformation with all the vigor I could muster. But neither the
New Leftism of my graduate-student days in the American North nor
the excitement of big-city anonymity and the chocolate-box assort-
ment of urbane pleasures, especially after my move to Toronto in
1969 to take a university teaching job—none of it quite did the trick.
Still living in Canada, mercifully out of teaching by 1974, becoming
the writer I'd always wanted to be and settling into marriage and the
mature rhythms of life and work, I found myself intellectually and

morally reconstructed only in part. To be sure, the speed of urban culture, its churn and liberty, had lost none of its charm. But whatever optimism I'd harbored about human emancipation from the bonds of history—including my own—or any but the most gradual social improvement was rapidly disintegrating.

In my private reading and conversation, without really being wholly aware of doing so, I had begun working down the syllabus of Modern pessimism, beginning with Nietzsche and continuing along the bookshelf through Heidegger and E. M. Cioran to Michel Foucault. In my more public career, I was increasingly fascinated by the experimental visual art of the 1970s—video and installation, painting and sculpture—which, like all lasting art, however "radical" its visual strategies or pretensions, was conservative in the philosophical sense. In common with all genuine conservatives—however hateful the word may have been, and still is, to creative people, especially since Reagan—the best contemporary artists of the last quarter-century have been hungry for reality as it is, the truth and grit and tooth of it, and impatient with the intolerant, avant-gardist dreams for reality's "improvement" imagined by the upbeat. As it happened, I was coming to certain conservative settlements with my times and culture—including a belief that escape from history is impossible, hence immoral to imagine; and the closely related ideas that we are most free precisely when engaged in tense, vigilant dialogue with our Western past, and in direst bondage precisely when trying to renounce our heirship to the West in general, and, more particularly, our necessarily vexed and vexing inheritance on the land, in the blood, of whatever specific place in the West each of us comes from.

I had carried such broadly Stoic ideas inside my head for many years before Aunt Vandalia's death—though, for whatever reason, I had never really recognized the connection between my thought and Southern culture. It was during the hurried toss of clothes and shaving gear into a suitcase, and while booking rush reservations on planes, that the link began to form in my mind, as I thought of Vandalia's fear of reaching the gates of heaven and being turned away, due to breach of honor. *That* was Southern. It was also a dreadful anxiety to take to one's deathbed. But were the costs and benefits of her commitment to the Southern way of living to be tallied up, would the sum be so very sad?

Vandalia had played the roles demanded of her by the elaborate set of unwritten codes governing the society she was born into. The respectability of Southern white folks, we might call it—a distinctive traditional path regulated largely by fear of public disgrace and hope of civic glory that can only be conferred, never bought. (Our Southern tradition knows much of shame, very little of guilt.) Her part had been performed well; and the little Southern town she served had rewarded her in its common coin: deference and admiration, and a reputation for good works, good conversation, and general virtue. I might not wish Vandalia's Southern life upon my daughter, born and reared an urban Canadian. But along with instilling in my aunt certain anxieties destined never to be resolved, the South had bestowed on her many years as rich as anyone can expect to receive, given life's inevitable suffering, and the very short distance anyone can turn within the indestructible narratives of identity imposed on us at birth.

In the hours before departing for the South to lay the old lady in the Southern ground, I found myself somehow already there, thinking of my Southern family, the land on which we had lived and died, and recollecting memories created over the generations of that enduring. I was not thinking of writing a book about such matters. What crossed my mind were only disparate ideas. The fact, for example, of how my personal trajectory over many years outside the South—from the relative intimacy of teaching to mass-media journalism (a kind of oratory), from a brief flirtation with optimistic Modernity into more durable Christian Stoicism, itself more cultural stance than enthusiastic religious ideal—how these moves had all been turns *toward* the South. Too, there was the fact of our fabrication, Aunt Vandalia's and mine, from the same family's blood and bones, the weaving of our lives, anxieties, obsessions, and fears on the loom of the same family.

And there was the recognition, emerging in my mind, of our common, dense belonging to the South, including the dread that's always part of such deep belonging. Where rules, rites, and codes create identity, after all, the danger of ritual defilement, and exclusion from the tribe, is ever present. For my aunt, her marriage to a divorced man may have entailed such pollution, though she would have to await Judgment Day to find out. As for me, I had been contaminated by Modernity and its culture of rootlessness and the New, and thought I had become a stranger to all worlds. But on the eve of the long flight south, I was no longer sure. Or, to put it a different way: I felt within me the first awakening to the old imperatives and inclinations of Southern culture. I was, after all the seasons lived in other places, other climates, other worlds of thought, still a Southerner; and I did not have to await God's verdict to find out *that*.

Because she feared death, Vandalia longed, while nodding off to sleep for the last time, to glimpse through her room's tall windows the pink crepe-myrtle blossoms intact or shattered by a late spring storm, their petals fluttering over the lawn she had let drift into wreckage, across the garden where her mother's roses now lay in ruin.

I knew what this dawn glimpse meant to her during her decline among the bedroom's walnut furnishings and sepia photographs and sacred books, between those walls papered in palest daffodil framed by dark paneling; for she had told me, in one of the few intimate conversations we had in her last year.

To look through the window and see the lawn, though no longer crisply kept—to see the rose garden, however blowsy and overgrown—was *not* to see her Maker, which meant her eternal fate was still unsealed. As I turned into the drive of her house on the day after hearing the news, the tires of my rented car crushed the flying petals of spring flowers, ever so important to her for her secret reason. It was then that sudden sorrow turned into the longer work of mourning, a lessening of the surprise death always brings, the return of calm.

As for the petals and unpruned trees, shrubs untended for seasons, all half-hidden in the pasture of weeds the lawn had become, the house itself—they would soon be free of the burden of melancholy reminding Aunt Vandalia had put on them, and perhaps even returned to a former joyfulness. The place had known much joy. John Matthew Mays, my grandfather, had built the frame house to his wife Erin's sociable, wise plans around 1910, not long after they and their two young children, Vandalia and John, my father, moved from Texas to the Louisiana farming community of Greenwood. What my grandmother wanted, and got, was a dwelling meant to

establish her husband's image as a solid merchant and entrepreneur
in a hamlet where ambitious newcomers were suspect—but to over-
state neither the image nor the ambition. Instead of putting up an
imposing American Victorian mansion, which the young couple
could have afforded, my grandmother designed a modern, simplified
arrangement of tall windows, ample porches, and long horizontal
roof lines, attractively fitting in among the houses of the established
Greenwood families. Inside, she connected the public areas—from
south verandah through living room and library to dining room—
with double doors kept shut in winter, but quickly openable for the
formal entertaining she expected to do, and did. The landscaping was
a poetic rhyming of traditional Southern plantings: shade-giving
pecans and low figs and taller chinaberry trees and mimosas, flower-
ing redbuds and fruit trees, nandina bushes with bright red berries,
and abounding roses. It was a house meant to impress, but quietly,
and to please the older families into which my grandmother wished
to knit her own.

Around 1930, only a couple of years after she and Uncle Alvin
were wed in front of the living room's brick fireplace, Vandalia
moved with her husband into John and Erin's house, and never
again lived elsewhere. It was only in later life that Vandalia began
letting both the house and its once-beautiful grounds gradually slide
toward the dereliction in which I found them. The neglect had
begun with the death of my grandmother, or Sister Erin, as she was
called by the townsfolk. To have called her Mrs. Mays, incidentally,
would have been to suggest you did not know her, which would
have been an insult, since everybody was *supposed* to know her. Sister Erin had long been elevated beyond the less laudatory *Miss* Erin,
the title Aunt Vandalia was accorded, in the entirely informal course
such matters take within small-town Southern culture.

It had always seemed that, when Sister Erin died in 1969, my
aunt felt not only the loss of her mother, but the departure of a certain glory that was not to be passed on to her. That dignity had long
lightened the house and its business—the conversations, unhurried
and warm as a bayou, among the men on the south verandah, and
the civil rites on the back porch, where Sister Erin, Miss Vannie, and
Alvin, who never got the honorific *Mr.* Alvin because the white
townsfolk never forgot he had long ago been my grandfather's

employee, ate grits and eggs on warm mornings. With Sister Erin gone, the fraying of the gardens began, on the outer perimeter.

There, just beyond the fence at the bottom of the farthest garden, stood and stands today a knightly oak, old and huge even in Aunt Vandalia's earliest girlhood photographs. Long before her father bought the land adjacent, the town's kids climbed and clambered among those heavy branches, anchored to its monumental trunk. The neighbor children owned the tree, as children own things, by loving and using them. My father—another in a long line of Mays boys named John—and Aunt Vandalia, both born in Texas and new to the upcountry Louisiana village, were quickly welcomed into the fellowship of the oak, without special privileges. And the oak itself opened its great limbs to them without discrimination, bestowing on little Vandalia and John exactly the same scrapes and falls and bone cracks it delivered to all its valiant would-be conquerors. The old people in the village feared the oak, perhaps because they had forgotten the thrill and happy bruising of their own initiations into its august society, or because they remembered them too well. But nobody who ever owned that land put obstacles in the path of the children, who were the oak's children.

Until the time of Aunt Vandalia, that is. Her suspension of access to the oak—the easiest access was across her property—was not intentional. The children's path to the tree merely became overgrown, and the bright margins around its cool penumbra of shade filled up with thorny shrubs. The abounding arcs of summer blackberry canes and wild roses quickly thickened into a home to poisonous vipers fond of the sweet fruit and grouchy about interlopers. In the spring Vandalia took her last leave of the house, the oak seemed very distant and isolated behind its infested, witchy barricades—forlorn, if a tree can be forlorn, due to the long absence of small visitors.

By the time I arrived for the burying, the decline begun at this far tree on the boundary had advanced inward to consume almost all the property. The rose garden, the chicken yard and summer garden—words that still call to mind childhood hours passed making tunnels among towering tiger lilies, and dead-heading the climbing roses with my aunt—had gone to weed. The one consoling thought in this moment was that all this wreck of roses, this misery of gardens would soon be past. In time, the grounds and house might be restored to the loveliness conferred on the site by Sister Erin. Once they were sold, I would never again have to see the oak, or the gardens or the grounds as they had become, or the untidy drapes of honeysuckle vines on low iron fences needing paint. The liberation from neglect would begin after the emptying of the house, and its sale to owners eager to reconstitute the old home's modestly refined beauties. But even before all that came to pass, I would, or imagined I would, be set free of certain feelings—surely temporary, I told myself—melancholy, odd. The rekindled memories would go, and with them the ancient and undefined awe that came with being there, on native Southern ground.

The week after the burial was taken up largely with legal paperwork and with readying the house for the caretaker, a young cousin who had kindly agreed to look after the place, but had no place to put his socks. Vandalia's companion through her last illness took up the job of clearing and cleaning rooms for him to live in, while I steeled myself for the infinitely larger job of going through and cleaning out all the house's stuffed nooks and corners. There was the pantry to empty, which Vandalia had often vowed to clean out and never did. And there were cartons of family papers, and trunks of pretty party dresses worn under glowing Japanese lanterns most of a century before.

And there was the attic to be sorted out, its myriad closets and drawers unlocked. The large, high room was heavy with dust settled over generations and ready to blow up into a choking cloud at the least breath. The shiny black dirt-daubers, too, were busy, flying in and out of their little adobe apartments under the rafters; and I loved them, and all else about the attic. When a child on visits, I had been allowed to play there only occasionally. I was also permitted to browse through the books and toys stacked on open wooden shelves—although Aunt Vandalia might have put a stop to such poking and exploring had she remembered she'd stowed there the sexological manuals my grandmother had given her before her wedding. But, though I was given leave to play among the old steamer trunks piled in the attic, my opening one of them unattended was clearly, and forever, forbidden. Hence the suddenly keen anticipation as I turned the key in the rusty lock of the first trunk to be opened—and the letdown when it turned out to be full of dowdy winter coats with fur trim of Eleanor Roosevelt vintage, and now serving as mouse nests. Other trunks turned out to hold better trove. Uncle Alvin's World War One gas mask and bundles of love letters in faded sepia ink turned up, along with postcards gathered at the turn of the century by Sister Erin's brother Will from his worldwide network of pen pals; blueprints for the airplane my father, still a teenager, built from a $1,000 mail-order kit; business papers from a century ago; boxes and boxes of photographs, loose or pasted into albums.

So far, this was a treasure hunt, a boy's adventure in a mysterious treasure-house. It turned into something more than that later, after my wife had joined me for the excavation. We chanced upon a certain small lady's trunk I did not remember having seen before. Once its lid was up, the luggage looked even less interesting than the others I'd opened. All that was visible in it at first was a heap of rags. But no sooner had we begun to excavate the trunk than Margaret found the first baby, eyes shut and fast asleep. His nightdress was faded and water-stained. His bisque face was smudged from his blanket's rot. But beneath the smudges, his baby's hair was as glowingly tawny, his cheeks and solemn pout as pink, his two tiny front teeth as white as they had been when Aunt Vandalia grew up, and put him down in the attic for his longest nap.

As I raised the baby from his bed of tatters, his eyes suddenly, startlingly, opened. They were bright azure, and they sparkled with delight and surprise, as if he had been just awakened from an afternoon's sleep. My wife set the baby on a small wooden chair, then continued the dig—finding in this chest, and in others nearby, babies of china and babies of bisque, some quite grown-up-looking girls in party frocks, and one fine sailor boy, dressed for church ashore.

Once we had pulled from their dirty beds and awakened the sleeping dolls, a large party of some twenty-five, and marveled at them awhile, we concluded there was only one right thing to do. So we rooted in other trunks and small boxes in closets, until we found what we thought might be there: the set of tiny cups, the saucers wrapped in crumbling newspapers from the teens of this century, along with jam pot and milk pitcher and sugar bowl. In view of their deep sleep through seventy freezing winters and as many Southern summers, we decided the dolls' dirty faces and the odd mouse nips to their camisoles should be ignored. Only the most nakedly bereft members of our little party, now gathered in a circle around a little twig-legged table, should be refitted—if only in make-believe—with the fresh frocks and sailor suits Aunt Vandalia had given them. Then Margaret ceremoniously poured out, while I rolled round a doll-sized trolley stacked high with imaginary cakes, custards, and flans. And so it was, in the wilting heat of the attic, that the dolls had their first tea since they were put down for naps, at the other end of this violent century.

The dolls went to sleep in the attic when my father and aunt still lived in a shimmering bubble of wealth and youth, and adrift in the feckless languor that wealth can give young people coming of age. The house was still new then, rich in the sounds of piano, voice, and violin—Southern Victorian ideals of respectability made musical study de rigueur, even if, as in my family, nobody had any talent—and graced by an optimism that was hardly touched by the First World War. Still a day's journey over bad roads from Shreveport, on the Red River—today a half-hour trip on Interstate 20—the Green-wood my father buzzed over in his little airplane, or at least its white ascendancy, had been made prosperous by cotton and trade with the small farmers scattered on the Louisiana hills round about. To look back now through my family's scrapbooks and diaries is to glimpse a time busy with fancy-dress parties; much churchgoing and more village gossip; the ceremonial departures of my grandparents by railway for their wintering spot in south Texas, their things packed by black servants into boxes and steamer trunks; and their equally momentous returns.

The dolls had already been slumbering several years when the music in the house was muted by the Crash and ill health, which descended like twin angels of desolation at almost the same time. The dolls missed the misery that came to the house then, even as they missed the horrors and inhumanities of the century that had too soon, too utterly, lost its youthful innocence. If, while waking them, I had a moment of hesitation, it was not for their sakes. They were, after all, just so much clay and cloth and sawdust. It was for my sake that I halted. Their eyes and smiles spoke of lovely and innocent childhoods of a kind I had known almost nothing, and

reminded me of another childhood, which I spent half a lifetime trying to rinse from my mind.

It began as a boyhood in light, shining on the Louisiana cotton plantation of John Bass Mays, my father. Seen from the garden I played
in, the encircling skyline of dark trees and bared, low hills defined
that world. Beyond the bounds of it, in other places, lay pockets of
family; and beyond that, persons known to me as *Yankees*, and, farther still, a war that meant we had no chocolate at Christmas, and
little gasoline for trips to the nearest movie theater, in the Texas border town of Waskom, some fifteen miles distant on narrow, pocked
roads.

Between me and the boundary, where the sky met the Louisiana
dirt, stretched the fields of the farm we called Spring Ridge, punctu-
ated here and there by small islands of trees and thicket crossed by a
muddy, shaded stream named Spring Branch, and otherwise open to
the sun. All things that might enter or depart the bright disc of home
had to cross its distant edge; so the horizon was something I
watched.

I watched the comings and going of cars and trucks on the narrow roads that crossed at Spring Ridge. One day I watched a twisted
frame house rumble by slowly on a flatbed truck, like a float, on its
way to a new location. And I watched west from the crossroads
along the way to Texas, beginning about five miles from my father's
land—over toward where the cabins of the field hands, whom John
Mays would gather into the back of his truck at dawn for the day's
planting and hoeing, and, when the time came in summer, for harvesting the white cotton bolls. The eastward track led more definitely
out, ending at the Red River city of Shreveport and the house of my
mother's urban people. North, some ten miles along the ribbon of
road through fields and deep creek bottoms, was Greenwood and the
house of my grandparents John and Erin, of Aunt Vandalia and
Uncle Alvin. I never minded the bumpy trip over the potholed track
there, for I loved the house.

While the roads were fixed on my mind's map, each with its particular direction and meaning, the routes the birds and planets,
storms and stars traveled across the horizon changed continually.
The advancing phalanx of black, wind-driven clouds that heralded

the violent storms in spring and autumn could be seen advancing over the line from a great way off, some time before they drove me inside to safety, then battered the frame house, its windows firmly shuttered against the debris that swirled in the storm's heart. At dawn in summer, the ascendant sun pushed ahead of it a long procession of messengers over the landline—first a spreading glow, next gilt-flecked clouds, then a suffused, shadowless radiance in the sky, reflected in sparkling dew on the fields of cotton. Migrating butterflies and birds sometimes crossed the land within the circle of horizon; and against the distant landline sometimes moved shadowy forms that I knew were cows and mules, but pretended were the wild, talkative animals in my storybooks, come to visit.

But of those fugitive phenomena I remember vividly, however, none captivated my childhood's imagination more completely than day's ending. After supper in high summer, I would ramble alone back to a certain low knoll behind the house, to watch the hue and brilliance shifting chromatically over the horizon during the sun's slow sinking toward Texas, the west and night. Though I was then not six years old, I can recall the beauty of our homeplace at dusk almost exactly, and I can still hear in my mind the exquisite cacophony of cricket and frog songs arising from creek bottom and bramble patch within the warm radiance of Southern twilight. Only once, when very small, do I remember bolting away from the little hill before sundown and rushing back into the house, and that was to tell my mother I had seen God.

Nothing less dramatic than a divine apparition, I suspect, would have tugged me off the knoll into the house before dark. I did not like the house of my father and mother—or, to be more precise, I seemed unable ever to find a spot for myself within the human geometry of it. My parents were out of love with each other and unhappy, my two sisters were teenagers deeply uninterested in a troublesome little brother who'd come along late. During the hot seasons of tending and bringing in the cotton, when my father was still at home, and not yet away hunting in Mexico and California, we would sit in the living room at night listening to President Roosevelt's reassuring voice on the radio, which seemed to salve the tense silence. The strain between my parents vanished when John Mays went away on the autumn hunting trips he adored; then fell again, in the dark, disordered crevices between the people in the house, when he returned. The ratio between me and only one person who came daily under the roof of my father's house never changed. Her name was Essie Doris Anderson, or Essie De, as I knew her then, whose strong black arms caught me one summer afternoon, and held me back on the creek bank, and kept me from sinking forever down into the waters of Blue Hole on Spring Branch, which everyone knew was bottomless.

Such were the dense elements from which my boyhood idea of *South* was fashioned: the tension in a house, and the peace of quiet cotton fields at noon, the dark beloved arms of Essie De, the deep shadow under the trees lining Spring Branch, and the sky at daybreak, and the roads. As children do—or at least children like me—I experienced the world within my horizon to be the only world that was, or could be; and so thought our homeplace, with its weathers and human masks, streams and roads and buildings, was eternal.

History came hurtling into this timeless clearing in the late summer of 1947, when my father was killed in what some called an automobile accident, and others thought was murder. I was not told of his death or funeral until weeks afterward, when time came for the September return for second grade at Greenwood School, toward which I had rattled off each morning of the school year in a rickety bus driven by Mr. Sam, a neighbor. Then all on an early September day, with the abruptness of an autumn afternoon windstorm, my mother told me John Mays was dead. She then packed me into the backseat of the car and drove the twenty-five miles to my maternal Aunt Antoinette's house in Shreveport, where we were to live.

I cannot now recall what I felt in those moments of wrenching. I can remember neither tears nor sorrow—only a sudden void rising toward my face, like the dark unriffled surface of the Blue Hole the day I almost fell into it. This time even Essie De's arms were not strong enough to catch me—and I went on falling and falling until the falling slowed, then stopped, and I found myself adrift in a deep dream-place of a city's hard streets and sidewalks, and houses crowded along the streets, and among strangers. I blame my mother for nothing, least of all for the quick overturning of the world I had known. Left suddenly a widow with almost no financial resources and a small son, beset by my father's farming debts and a platoon of creditors demanding payment, she got in the harvest of cotton, then sold her late husband's cherished hunting rifles, rented the house, and sold all other plantation goods except the land. Not long after the last autumn cotton was harvested at Spring Ridge, she began to succumb to the cancer that eventually would take her life.

Though probably predisposed from birth to the chronic depression I have lived with all my life, the symptoms of the disease began to manifest themselves only then, in the extreme and disarraying interval between the deaths of father and mother. I despised and feared the city to which I'd been moved, and—as children often do following the disappearance or divorce of parents—I began to hate myself, morbidly and obsessively. By my eighth year, thoughts of suicide had become constant companions, and radical alienation from love, ground, and any upbearing certainty had emerged as my central experience of the world. But when not fixed on my worthlessness, and strategies of self-destruction—always, drowning in the Blue Hole—my thoughts turned inward to memories of Spring Ridge.

As it moved into the mental distance, the plantation of history became less true place than a fantastical Eden simplified and internalized, made perfect and brittle, by bleeding away all the colors that were ugly in the original fabric. The flaws of John Bass Mays I knew of—his infidelities, his alcoholism, his neglect of wife and family— gradually mended, and he was again, in my mind, the valedictorian, the shining lad in the tales told me after his death by Sister Erin and Aunt Vandalia. These mental transfigurations were hastened by the rapid envelopment of the real Spring Ridge's open farmland by bush, thick and ugly in a way peculiar to land once cleared and inhabited, then left to be retaken by the wild. In only a couple of years after my mother's abandonment of the farm, the horizon line had risen to the tops of quick-growing trees, and the once-open fields were invisible beneath the heavy gnarl and dark of shrub, tree, and vine. And gradually, at the same time, reality was withdrawing from me, including what reality I had known on the plantation—the cycle of celestial, earthly, and cultural phenomena that had constituted what certainties I knew in earliest years.

And because it was merely a flimsy illusion outside history, this mental construction I called Spring Ridge—the diseased glowing of an unsettled mind, memory tinged with alluring delusion—inflicted ever more desolate homelessness on my soul, a *strangeness* to the human world that I believed had betrayed me. In those hateful class-rooms in Shreveport schools, in the aloneness of my dark room in the house where my mother lay dying, I would swim in bright fantasies of a Southern boyhood in light, forgetting the reality of the world far overhead, up in the open world where things and people beloved had been snatched away by death, leaving me to drown in bottomless depths. There was only one person near at hand whom I allowed to touch me in this deep place of malignant remembering, and draw me out of it, if only for a moment—Essie De, who had come up from Spring Ridge to Shreveport to look after me as my mother's powers to do so leaked from her ravaged body.

With the dawn of adolescence a few years after she died, I began to be drawn inexorably by desire toward the human world that frightened me; but, rather than allow that pull from illusion to run its healing course, I suffocated desire for all else save the fantastical past. My decision at age fouteen to run away from the care of my maternal aunt in Shreveport and seek refuge with my grandmother, Aunt Vandalia, and Uncle Alvin in Greenwood sprang from this longing to sink yet deeper into the only past I trusted. Weekend visits there had been the only gracious openings in a childhood otherwise hemmed in by thickets of unhappiness. I loved the house from top to bottom—from the mysterious attic and my father's many-windowed bedroom on the same upper floor, to the verandah on which my grandfather and his planter friends and neighbors had sat on summer evenings, smoking cigars and talking politics and cotton. I loved the house where Sister Erin and my aunt told stories.

Among other people, they told stories of my father, and of his valiance, inventiveness, habitual kindliness. The stories were not meant to deceive me; but they deceived us all. And gradually I began to believe that only here, in the house where my father had been a radiant boy—among his books, in his room adorned with the mum-mified heads of the big game animals he killed as a man—could I be a Southern boy like him. Aunt Antoinette tried to stop me from leaving Shreveport, and so did Essie De; but I would not be stopped. My last two years of public education were completed at Greenwood School. And yet the fall into confusion did not stop throughout those two years, but only intensified in rate of descent.

During my early twenties, as part of my last attempt to protect the lesion of nostalgia gnawing on my soul, I threw my whole heart into *being Southern*, in the sense I understood the phrase—living in an archaic and presumably noble past that was as out of step with present-day America as I was out of step with reality. I had the very good fortune to collapse under the intolerable burden, and to fall, not into another fathomless Blue Hole, but into the care of a wise and compassionate New York psychiatrist.

For years after that kindly disaster, I thought little about my past in the South, and reminisced not at all. The reason lay, at least in part, in an awareness of the peculiarly *Southern* cast of my childhood self-punishment—the poisoned vision of corrupted innocence that informed it, the obsessive posturing and withdrawal into fantasy that accompanied it. Our history since 1865 has made Southerners prone to this strategy. We are not, of course, the only Modern people to have launched a rebellion against the world to preserve a doomed ideology compounded of racism and tyranny, and been crushed on the field of war. That historical experience Southerners share with the German people in the twentieth century. And like the Germans after both their modern defeats, many white Southerners in the generations after the Civil War found themselves with no fixed place on any map. Hence, the manufacture of such visionary ideals as the *Old South* and the *Lost Cause*—and hence, the unreality that has long lain thick, like fog, in the hollows and bottomlands of Southern imagination. I had become ill by drinking the infected waters all around me; by *being Southern* in the dark sense of wounded, lamed by history and by hankering after lost worlds.

But if I did not *think* of myself as a Southerner very often, the truth that I was and am one had begun to return with peculiar urgency from the moment I heard of Aunt Vandalia's death. This sense of kinship with a region, and a certain tribe there—in my case, white and ancient, bound by generations of farming to the seasons and the ground—is not, of course, necessarily warm and welcome; and to experience one's community in blood with the living and the ancient dead as *comforting* is certainly to misunderstand all that genealogy has to teach. The calls that issue from the known past of any family are stern: to renew a taut dialogue with the ancestors, drawing what treasures are to be found in their lives and deeds, rejecting the rest, always in a spirit of reluctant *pietas* for the legacy and example of our dead.

On the day in the attic when we uncovered the dolls, I found myself surrounded with witnesses to tenderness, delight, and youthfulness I'd never known in my immediate family at Spring Ridge, and known little of in Greenwood. I had long thought of my grand-mother as eternally old and ill and distant, Aunt Vandalia as always weary. But the dolls spoke of *another* Vandalia, with young eyes that gleamed as theirs did. I had believed, until then, that I knew Van-dalia—only to be told by the dolls and the lovely shine of unearthed teacups, and the "memory books" into which she'd tucked a girl-hood's dance cards and letters and photos, that I knew very little.

Other than my mental picture of Aunt Vandalia, what else about my Southern history had I similarly, wrongly simplified? Quite a lot, I later began to suspect. I had become one of those rushing people who, over many years, gradually forgets who he was, from what his-tory he had come, from what precincts of imagination. But I had also been someone who *must* forget a boyhood that had become warped and oppressive, in order to have a manhood with any freedom or love in it—and, thereafter, a man practiced in keeping a safe distance from the tomb of forgetfulness, to avoid waking memories best left sleeping. And, surely, had Vandalia died earlier, when I was still pulling myself out of mental illness, building a career and a family—or had she died later, when I was old and lost in the trivial hobbies of the old—I might have quickly disposed of all that reminded me of the Southern past of my family, and my roots in that soil. But Aunt Vandalia's death came in the middle of my life, just before fifty, at a time men are peculiarly prone to thinking of what might have been. It was in such a frame of mind—in the moments of painful thought following news of Vandalia's death and, later, among those brittle photographs, boxes of memoirs and memorabilia, old clothes and dolls and other reminders of familiar lives lived in the Southern past—that I began to hear the call of the South's beauties, complexi-ties, and contradictions, and decided to seek the source of that dis-tant and enchanting music, echoing in the deep places of what I am.

The work of writing, Milan Kundera has said, is not to proclaim truth, but to discover it. My intention in beginning this work, and in pursuing it, was to discover the truth of the South—at least the truth of dwelling on the Southern land embodied in the ten generations of my ancestors and kin who have lived there. This is not a work of general Southern history, for I am not competent to write such a book, nor a celebration of the foods and games and other oddments that together constitute the academic pastiche known as Southern Culture. It is not a compilation of family stories and genealogical connections. While creating such volumes is an honorable and worthy task, it has never held much interest for me. *Power in the Blood* is a work without a thesis or moral, without speculations about "whither the South." Of proposals for agrarian revival, Dixie spiritual remedies for what's ailing the Greater Republic, Old South nostalgia or New South strategies, and so on, the world already has many, and will doubtless have many more; but I lack the political wisdom to add to that stack, even if I wished to do so.

What I have written is the record of walking a path toward a beauty I had almost lost. By *path*, I mean exactly that: *a ways to go*, as Southerners say—a distance, an interval between what we know and do not know, and a path, above all, of *thinking*. It is not a way out, or up to something better. Whatever truth is in it lies not in where the path takes us, but in the walking of it—in learning what it was and is to be human *in a certain way*. For Southerners, that way has always been defined by memory and the land; so, in traversing Southern landscape, remembered and present, I have tried to keep on the trail that moves closest to the contours of hills and creek bottoms. In common with all genuine tradition, the Southern path receives its authority from those who walk it, and find it good.

Starting out on the path was not hard. When lost in the Labyrinth with the Minotaur on his scent, Theseus had only to pick up the end of Ariadne's thread, which is everywhere, to find his way out. So I stooped down, and found the dolls; Margaret and I gave them tea, and that was the beginning. The oldest of the old greeted me there—memories from deep time, setting me on the first steps out on this voyage through the peculiar, papery, lonesome country of the past. For Theseus, the route through the Labyrinth was outbound, and so, in a sense, was mine. It took me from the attic in Greenwood, where I was first prompted to recollection, to reading the narratives written by kinsmen and listening to the old tales told in my family, and, later, to journeys across the Southern hills and

The children's tree, Greenwood

low-country lands on which this family has lived and worked for upward of four hundred years.

In walking the Southern path, I discovered how deeply I belong to that way, to the Southern sky and land and history, and its mythic permutations and shifting truths. A Southerner can leave behind the landscape, and the twice-told tales, and the deeper wisdom whispered by our land's gullies and broad fields. One can attempt, as I did, unsuccessfully, to become wholly reconciled to the industrial and technical culture of the Modern era, and take a comfortable place within the mechanical civilization that now threatens the earth and humankind's fragile tenure on it. Yet, at certain times, we meet strangers on this trail of forgetfulness, who turn out to be *ourselves*, prompting us to return to the path, if only for a while, and learn from it. For the path itself is the oldest of the old coming forward to greet and teach us, to invite us to take up again the sparing of our tradition, the saving of our intimate histories, the stories of our ground and blood.

But those matters lie some way from where we are now, still in memory's attic. As Hilda Doolittle reminds us in a beautiful poem:

now is the time to re-value
our secret hoard

in the light of both past and future,
for whether

coins, gems, gold,
beakers, platters,

or merely
talismans, records or parchments,

explicitly, we are told,
it contains

for the scribe
which is instructed,

things new
and old.

PART ONE

OUR INWARD TRACE

1

The Bow and the Lyre

Courthouse, Hampton

ONE BRILLIANT AUTUMN HALF A LIFETIME AGO, I TRAVELED through Mississippi's red-dirt hills, to the county town of Oxford. The little city sat prim on her ridge in those days, dressed in the same lace of peeling white shutters she had worn for a century, waiting in her parlor for the gentleman caller of New South industry and commerce, who would never step up on the porch and knock.

So she told stories. In that regard, Oxford was not unlike myriad little towns dotting old farming country from the Carolinas into Texas, and not much different from a dozen I'd known in my Louisiana childhood. The folk and families in them all had their stories, and exchanged them on verandahs, invented more by hearthsides or campfires, wrote them in diaries, proclaimed them in sermons and Pioneer Days speeches, and passed them, parent to child, down the generations. There were whispered stories about names fading on the middle pages of massive family Bibles, and stories of the locals, informally understood to represent something more than *just* local. Exaggeration was part of the rhetorical style. In a Southerner's retelling of any tale, every farm becomes a plantation, I recall reading somewhere; every elderly man "a gentleman of the old school," every widow a saint, every notable disgrace or rise a grave moral *exemplum*.

But if inclined to exaggerate and allegorize more than the common run of humankind, rural Southerners do, or did, come by this inclination honestly, just by growing up in a popular culture saturated by biblical stories of epic heroism, vast and sobering loss, of huge wickedness punished, and of Old Testament struggles for righteousness ending, too often, in tragic disappointment. These aren't the only stories in the Bible, of course; nor did their Hebrew authors intend them to be read as Southerners, black and white, tended to read them. But they were the tales that proved durably attractive to the Southern imagination, still pessimistic and moralistic well into this century, long after American culture generally had become one of optimistic hedonism and practicality. It all had to do with the steeping of that imagination in the Classics.

The Southern mind's establishment in the Greek and Roman writers began with the birth of Southern culture itself, when the first English immigrants arrived in the seventeenth century, and it took a remarkably long time to erode. Cicero's dialogues on friendship, duty, and other attributes of a gentleman were being drilled into Southern boys past the dawn of the twentieth century. Before vanishing, however, the ancient writers had done a remarkable job of shaping Southern sensibility by defining Southern pedagogy. It was incongruous by the time I got to high school. But though the girls in my high school sported plastic-sprayed bubble hairdos and bras shaped like nuclear missile prows, and the boys remorselessly greased and combed their hair to make it glint like Elvis's, we still studied Latin, learning to read Julius Caesar's flat, factual prose, along with ennobling bits of Horace and Catullus. Such training may seem strange now, but we kids in the 1950s did not find it so. One afternoon, I recall, Latin class was halted temporarily by the wail of thermonuclear attack sirens. As trained to do during such Cold War drills, we immediately slapped our books shut, crawled under our desks, and stayed there until the all-clear sounded. Whereupon we crawled out, everyone reprimped his or her elaborately constructed hairstyle, then we went back to puzzling out a patch of Ovid's *Metamorphoses*. Nobody found the elements of this event wildly incongruous, as they were, largely due to the talent all kids have for ignoring adult oddity and carrying on. At least part of our accommodation, however, had to do with being small-town Southern in the 1950s, which involved the daily negotiation of cultural pluralities and incongruities—TV soap operas and old family stories, rock 'n' roll and Sunday school, and the other ironies of everyday life typical of any hierarchical culture.

Even in their decline as teachers of the good life, the Roman writers were still shaping the way we thought. Mine was perhaps the last generation of Americans to grow up believing education was principally a matter of learning to live virtuously, by imitating virtuous examples, rather than acquiring a trade. We may not have been aware that Livy compiled a set of biographical paradigms for young Romans to conform their lives to, that in turn had set the standard for Western education for the previous millennium, or that our Southern schools were among the last redoubts of such ideals, anywhere in the West. It hardly mattered. Southerners had long been accustomed to reading everything, especially the most popular ancient book, the Bible, in the way Livy prescribed. "The study of history is the best medicine for a sick mind," he wrote; "for in history you have a record of the infinite variety of human experience plainly set out for all to see; and in that record you can find for yourself and your country both examples and warnings; fine things to take as models, base things, rotten through and through, to avoid." Since the rise of civil rights, perhaps partly because of it, otherworldly apocalyptic enthusiasm or comfortable American liberalism has everywhere displaced the essentially pagan, tragic resignation once at the heart of Southern popular education and religion. But as recently as my first trip to Oxford, when Martin Luther King was thundering for righteousness and the Kingdom of God as splendidly as any Hebrew prophet—even that late, no people on earth would have disagreed more vehemently than Southerners with Hegel's proposition that the one thing history teaches is that nobody ever learns anything from history.

We do learn from what has gone before, or can, so the theory goes; but because we are inwardly blind, the truth must be proclaimed in great rhetorical images that know our heart's location, seek it out, lodge there; hence the supreme place accorded preaching and political oratory in the South. Viewed against the background of Southern civilization, the writing of William Faulkner is a late, brilliant fluorescence of the traditional regional tendency to see stern destiny unfolding in each event, however ephemeral, and to behold in every story a Plutarchian (or Æsopian) *it just goes to show!*—perhaps, indeed, the glorious sunset of an American imaginative style, all but vanished today. But at the time of my first visit to Faulkner's homeplace—with the writer in the ground only a year, and his books at the zenith of fame in the literary world—Faulkner was the very revelation of Oxford, the South, the world in its tragic becoming and passing away. In 1950, a bit more than a decade before his death, Faulkner had been catapulted by the Nobel Prize from popularity into inevitability, transposed from the "regionalist" book list over to the American Literary Canon, thence into the university seminars, where his art became fodder for scholarly papers without number. But he had come to embody, for a world readership, this revelation by transmuting Oxford's parlor tales and hunting-camp talk into parables of deepest human existence, and passed them on from Oxford into all humankind's passionate thought. I went to Oxford that first time because of Faulkner, to seek the lanes that had become thoroughfares in narrative, the buildings, faces, and intervals between what Faulkner had raised from elements in local knowledge into figures in writing's turbulent geography.

By that time, while studying at a Northern university, I had become chronically obsessed with making and keeping myself Southern in the archaic, anti-American sense, which in turn skewed my earliest readings of Faulkner's works. I pored over *Go Down, Moses* and *Absalom, Absalom!* for messages from the deep time of the Southern ancestors, to which I wanted to return—surely the worst frame of mind in which to read anything. Yet I was studying majestic literature, which, like all great art, has a way of inspiring discontent with our narrow, rushed lives, and calling us into the encounters with larger mental and emotional life that such art celebrates.

For many people, in every age, the word-pictures in books have satisfied this yearning—though there have always been folk who've left the storyteller's fire or shut their books in discontent, and had to travel. It's at least as old as the Babylonian *Epic of Gilgamesh,* but certainly much older—this impulse to go in search of lost legendary worlds, exotic fastnesses, Eden and Shangri-La. When I was coming of age, and though I knew nothing of them, the novels of Jack Kerouac were doing that for an American generation slightly older than mine. Myriad young Americans were in their cars, on the road, harvesting memories, getting the kicks denied them by the straighter-laced 1950s.

My voyage to Oxford was to be dismally more tame than those of the Beats—tourism, that is, of a serious, reserved sort, common among literary students of my time. As I wrote in my diary at the time of my trip to Faulkner's Oxford, "I descend to the realm of shades to offer sacrifice and seek wisdom of the *genius loci.*" To get the spirits talking, of course, involved knowing the rites, and faithfully performing them. As a Faulkner-besotted reader who'd been to Oxford before me said, the first station on the *via* was The Grave, a plain plot on the sprawl of hill called St. Peter's Cemetery, where Oxford has always buried her dead. There we were to offer the usual sacrifice to the *manes* of the departed: a fifth of whiskey, Kentucky's finest sour mash bourbon or some lesser kind, depending on the munificence of one's fellowship that year.

The next stopping place was the shaded gate of Rowan Oak, the small antebellum manor Faulkner bought in 1930 for no down payment and $75 a month. The road in was posted by a conspicuous *No Trespassing* sign—though the turbid gloom of the place would probably have slowed trespass without the sign. Dense stands of cedar and scrub oak gathered too close against the house, and the formerly sunny field lands and lawns had been snatched back into shadow by the green force that everywhere seems very close to the surface of the rural South. Though its abjection was not yet complete in the 1960s, the land around Rowan Oak was infused by the peculiar savagery one finds in places that once were tame. The vines were too thick, the magnolia blossoms too massive and fragrant, the once-tidy approach for carriages and cars now forlorn between margins of encroaching weed. Up the lane, in the white house just visible behind magnolias and shrubbery, dwelt Faulkner's widow, Miss Estelle. I could imagine her, because I had known other women like her: Southern wives who had passed their lives in the shadow of a famous husband, their pain unheard, unshared; who, upon being widowed, could not then step out of the absent shadow, but drew darkness around themselves ever more tightly. Of Southern women who made their famous art without men looming over them—Flannery O'Connor, Carson McCullers, Eudora Welty—we know a great deal. Southern women who made no art, but lived with difficult men who did, seem to leave less than nothing—a trace of dust where once a woman existed, a rumor; nothing more.

What fantasies pilgrims from outside the South nurtured about the widow's tiny world behind the gate of Rowan Oak, I do not know. But it came as no surprise when, twenty-five years later—Miss Estelle dead, the mansion turned into a shrine in the keeping of the University of Mississippi—I found its rooms rich in things, and the sorts of things, I recognized from my grandfather's house. The complete Dickens, for instance, stacks of Ellery Queen novels, speeches of Franklin D. Roosevelt in gold-stamped bindings—and a black Underwood typewriter, buck heads mounted over the fireplace, Scram Dog Repellent Bomb and horse liniment in the back gallery, undiscarded bottles of used-up patent medicine in the bathroom closet. All this was still out of reach when I first stood by the gateway of Rowan Oak, but I knew what fragrances and ornaments must be in such a house, because they had been in my grandfather's.

If they are little more than evocative props kept in the literary shrine today, and collectibles in yard sales across the South, such artifacts recalled a traditional Southern world, of cotton plantation and small town, and an almost Japanese sense of decorum and deference, that I had known only in its decline. It had been a world rooted in racial injustice and black misery; those cultural foundations were among the hateful Southern things forever troubling my slide into spiritual archaism. But my keenest thoughts at the gates of Rowan Oak, on that first visit, were of fragrances that provoked memories—the resinous odor of cooking-fire pine smoke in the clothes of my father's black farmhands, and the flowery perfume worn by the ladies in white dresses who would come calling at the house at dusk, the South of village life and settlement, all of it passing into unreality.

The next stop—a beholding of Faulkner's memorabilia at the University of Mississippi—was easier, and more interesting, because it involved an expectation of the Ordeal. I'd heard that no trip to Oxford could be thought consummated without a memorable bark or reprimand or flat turn-down of some request from Miss Oldham. She was both curator of the university collection and Estelle Oldham Faulkner's sister. And in her quasi-tribal role as vestal keeper of the legacy—and, like other Southern spinsters I'd known, unaccustomed to backtalk from anybody—Miss Oldham felt free to avenge her hidden sister's pain on us pilgrims, come to honor this no-count Oxford drunk whom dread Fate had made her brother-in-law. To feel that lash was to stand, if only for a moment, within the circle of conflicted emotions Oxonians felt about their native cosmopolite and local curiosity, their outrageous boozer and greatest celebrity. Miss Oldham possessed power to give us a sense of the feelings the writer had inspired, thereby becoming a legend, even a monument, in her own right.

I see nothing wrong with such literary touring. Nor was there anything unusual in traveling hundreds of miles to visit a grave and to be snapped at by Miss Oldham. Such dandyism was simply part of being a literary student in America during the early years of the 1960s—before, that is, the proper study of writing turned from exegesis and philology into philosophical interrogation, intended to torment a text or utterance until it goes mad and denounces itself. We had not yet heard of Jacques Derrida or deconstruction or the undecidability of text and truth. The American academic fascination, at least in the English departments, with Roland Barthes and structuralism was close at hand but still a ways off; and multicultural, feminist, and similar studies of the marginalized were largely unimagined. We believed not only that the Literary Canon did and must exist, but that the works in it were *sacred* texts in an almost technical, theological sense; an anticanon, like that of the early Christian heretic Marcion, to the list of biblical books we memorized in Sunday school. We believed the reading of Shakespeare and Tolstoy and Faulkner could unshackle a soul of its deadly provincialism and make it universal.

While my thinking has been enriched over the years by Derrida's writing and the mischief of philosophers and writers in his school, I am glad to have done my graduate work in the rather old-fashioned time I did, and to have believed what I believed, and to have left academia before the culture of literary studies changed. We could still gather again in the common room of an autumn evening and, without self-consciousness, swap tales of our travels as though nobody had ever traveled before—tales of tears shed at Pound's grave behind the yews ringing Venice's mortuary island of San Michele, of awe upon seeing the tomb of Virgil on the road to Puteoli, or, those being the last days of genteel literary Leftism, of a stiffening of spine before the monstrous bust of Marx in Highgate Cemetery.

Essie De, mammy to all the children in my father's household, has told me I talked about going to New York when I was four, still playing in the cotton patch and chasing rabbits to the edge of the blackberry thickets. I had read *Huckleberry Finn*, and decided to build a raft on the muddy bank of a nearby bayou and drift down to the Red River, thence to New Orleans, and *then* go to New York. Eventually, of course, I did leave the South, to study, and in the North encountered the Modern European writers, artists, and filmmakers who were already worrying my obsessive Southernness. I was already on the road, that is, to Modernity, and that vision was exposing and wounding my desire for roots in the Southern land and history. Due largely, I believe, to these quickening doubts, the standard tour of Faulknerian sites turned out to be a joyless chore. I did the circuit perfunctorily, picked up some routine stories to relate, then abandoned the track. The next step was to gather my things and leave—a step half-taken, leaving a suitcase half-packed on the bed and me exhausted. Without desire or strength to go out or to stay in my hotel room, I found myself on the streets, walking without design, unthinking, merely seeing.

There were few people about. The wicker chairs on verandahs of the South Lamar Street mansions, maidenly relics from a long-past season of local wealth, had been emptied by autumn heat, and even the avenue was empty of foot traffic, even after the sunshine had begun to fail. In that quiet, the light seemed to sadden the flamboyant gingerbread embellishments imposed on plain Classical façades. The slanting glow rinsed white columns and porticos in bone-gray tint, moist and diffuse—a strange illumination of architecture that had been invented under the dry blue heavens of Greece.

Back on the square, where my hotel was, the people there for afternoon business were disappearing with the day. Farmers, come up that morning from the Yocona River bottom in their mule-drawn wagons to buy seed and offer the autumn harvest for sale on Oxford's central square, rattled away down the hill falling away from the square. The seed outlets that smelled of earth and sky, the hardware store fragrant with machine oils and turpentine, closed their doors one by one, and their proprietors walked home to supper. Old men, who had been gaming and talking in the shade of the Lafayette County Courthouse, packed their dominoes and left the benches, fading away down the streets. Electric lights flicked on behind yellowing paper shades or swags of drape in the houses just off the square; and night came to Oxford.

Though more of them exist now, there were several things a young stranger could do on the night streets of Oxford—bars worth prowling, for instance, if only to catch the brawls that broke out in them each evening, redneck against redneck in a rite of boozing, whoring, and fighting. Another Southern ceremony I could have performed, hemmed in by as many thorny vines of custom and code as the bar fight, was *visiting*. It had been something learned in childhood, this art of the visit—something never forgotten, once incised on mind, manner, and attitude. But with no one to visit, and not inclined to do so in any case, I walked back to my room and took a place beside the high, dusty window.

Peace came with Oxford's nightfall, and the nightly vigil. With lights off in the room, I sat wondering and looking through those panes, and waiting for images of the square to emerge and slide, overriding but not displacing one another, like transparencies layered and back-lit. There was the quotidian square, now almost empty except for a few University of Mississippi students shortcutting their way across it, and the odd car skirring around its unpoliced corners. The only light was shed by street lamps and some leaks of radiance from the closed business establishments defining each of the square's sides. The silent pronouncement made by the square's architecture was victory—of modern trade over ancient poverty, law over chaos, style over barbarism. Tall, ornate Victorian storefronts framed the town's center then, as they do today. Neilson's department store, its broad arcade sheltering the sidewalk from rain; the elegant Victorian façade of the United Southern Bank; a jewelry store decorated with a luxurious flourish of oak-leaf-and-acorn grillwork worthy of New Orleans in the *belle époque:* all affirmed the postbellum triumph of trade, the resurgence of wealth in the wake of defeat. To Southerners, not God, went the glory: no steeple rose over the square, and Oxford's churches had taken no part in creating its architecture. Dominating the square's margin were the stores, law offices, and institutions of government that had always anchored Oxford's life to its long ridge.

All the glass fronts of these establishments faced inward, drawing eye and mind to what stood at their focus, on the town's highest point: the little Palladian étude enshrining the justice of Lafayette County. Faulkner had used the building in *Requiem for a Nun* as the model for the courthouse of his fictional Yoknapatawpha County. "The center, the focus, the hub," he called it, "musing, brooding, symbolic and ponderable, tall as cloud, solid as rock, dominating all. . . ." But the architecture seemed more tentative than rocklike—primly civilized and small. Surely, it celebrated in sturdy Corinthian column and clean, virtuous line the happy fruits of justice—though no one could reasonably call *this* building tall as cloud, dominating all.

If the courthouse's charming formality called anything sharply to mind, it was the destruction required for such founding and raising. In Classical architecture, wrote Nietzsche, "beauty entered the system only secondarily, without impairing the basic feeling of uncanny sublimity, of sanctification by magic or the gods' nearness. At most the beauty was tempered by *dread*—but this dread was the prerequisite everywhere." The structure appeared in my midnight thoughts in that way: as an unintended cenotaph to the vanished forests that once shaded its open site, the vanquished bear and wolves that once roamed Oxford's ridge, the Chickasaw people, dispersed after their cession of the site to American newcomers in 1830, the forgotten blacks whose energies were enslaved to raise such courthouses from their rigid quadrangles in small towns across the South. Violence found its expression in the Classical courthouse, as in all buildings of its sort, by the deliberate *absence* of victims—the absence of great forest animals, of trees long ago hacked down to open the square's site to the sky, where once America's vast arboreal shadow shrouded everything.

Only one of Oxford's dead, a slender soldier erect on his high plinth, was explicitly commemorated on the square. Though he'd been there in the corner of my eye all along, I had kept watch on the square several nights before I actually *saw* him. The beautiful stone man—every lad and man and boy who defended the South in schism—seemed to me a second Dionysius who could live again, and forever, as long as his memory remained vivid and true. "And when their fated end comes," wrote Xenophon of fallen warriors, in words the men of postbellum Oxford would have known by heart, "they do not lie forgotten and without honor, but they are remembered and flourish eternally in men's praises." On the square was an image of this warrior, the resurrected Dionysius—the essential spirit of the South, the imperishable truth found in fragments after the husk of the Southern republic had been torn away—found, and reassembled in the hearts of those who erected the statue. As the inscription has it: "The sons of veterans unite in this justification of their fathers' faith."

But what was this faith, requiring vindication? Or, to be more precise, what did the fathers invest faith *in*? Men will die in battle for the ideal of a racist society, because it is an image, if a perverse one, of true homeland, a citadel of honor and stability. Men have always been willing to die on the battlefield for an idea or a feeling, but rarely, if ever, for what they understood to be a business arrangement. If, then, the sacred idea remaining after the Confederacy's fall was not slavery, but something worthy of our remembrance, what was it?

That night, for the first time since arriving in Oxford, I began to feel the South as something other than a memory, but as a presence under my feet, close at hand, *within*. It was as though a key had turned in a long-locked door, which then swung open into the ominous darkness. There waited the true thing that had been mediated for years by fragrances and childhood memories, both gilded and terrible, embodied in the stone soldier on the square, yet somehow separable from both my memories and from stone. I thought I should never feel its nearness; that, if alive anywhere, this evasive idea lay sleeping under Southern malls and the American expressways spanning the South, beneath the great postwar suburbs ringing every Southern city, under the avalanche of televised, standardized *American* imagery.

A true, final descent into the South—meaning what, I did not know, or want to know—suddenly became repulsive; and soon my bags were packed and latched, the hotel bill paid, my car's nose pointed north toward Memphis, and beyond. Returned, in front of the fire in the graduate common room, literary travelers unrolled carpets of happy memories. Having none, I unrolled lies of Oxford, and of what it was to be there. Were I then a sensible man, or at least confident in the Modernity I'd achieved, I might have faced squarely the sensuous feelings aroused one night in Mississippi, the nagging oddity (at least in my view) of the inscription on the stone soldier's plinth and tried to uncover the curious power in this episode. As it happened, no such face-off was to occur that autumn, or for some years thereafter. The unfading worry about *what lay outside the door* in the Oxford darkness was soon dragged into the cauldron of worries I was becoming, to the exclusion of all other emotions, and even sustained thought. The accumulated legacy from a lifetime of disruptions—the deaths of parents, wrenchings from one home to another—were overwhelming and deadening any ability I might have had to reason my way back to Oxford, and puzzle out the oracular presence I felt there. A year from that autumn, I could no longer read, study, even *listen*; whereupon I lost my mind.

Long before the time came to close Aunt Vandalia's house, I had found it again, and was well up the slope (which has no summit) toward sanity. I had found a good life far from the South, and a new career, as a journalist, to replace the one that failed. As far as I could tell, the sharpest jolts of my life's first half were past; I was now settled into the gentler rhythms of middle age, and settled into the forgetfulness of origins that had come with my truce with Modernity. Or so I thought, until the climb into the attic with my wife, and the encounter with the abandoned dolls, and with the other quietly beautiful things in that dusty place, all calling out to the depths of what I had always been. It certainly never occurred to either of us that anything there could pull me, as indeed was to happen, back to Oxford, and into the conversation with the Mississippi town left unfinished twenty-five years before.

Among the discoveries in the attic was a bulky cardboard box stuffed with brittle clippings, letters written in fading ink, photocopies, nearly illegible scribblings on foolscap pages. At first glance, I recognized nothing of importance, certainly nothing worth keeping. The papers heaped into the carton seemed to be yet another clutterly pile of items Aunt Vandalia called her "things"—inchoate stuff she always *meant* to arrange, but never got around to doing. Weary of excavating the attic, imagining we had found most of what was worth cherishing, I almost threw out the box. But finding the dolls tucked away in dilapidated chests had made me wary, so I decided to do a quick examination of the contents, just to be sure. The dusty carton, I discovered, contained the leavings of my aunt's intense, disorderly ten-year research on our Southern family's lineage and history.

Aunt Vandalia, I knew, had become interested in such matters in the early years of the 1960s, when she was nearing fifty. She had worked at them for about five years, until Sister Erin's last illness took her mind off most everything else. It was during this hard time that the harvest was boxed and dispatched to the attic. Neither the inaugural date of this investigation, nor the method of its pursuit, is surprising. Vandalia's desk, piled high with genealogical documents and with letters answered and yet unanswered, was only one island in an archipelago of such desks, scattered then across the South between Charleston and Dallas. These were uneasy years for Southern white men and ladies of my aunt's age and circumstances. Many had been quietly appalled by the shifts in American postwar culture—the engulfing of their isolated rural towns by vast suburbs and strangers, the disruption of their mainline churches' traditional restraint by either impossible Modernist latitude or intolerable evangelical enthusiasm, the decline of the New Deal social establishment (to which Aunt Vandalia's father had belonged, as merchant and politician) and the rise of such strange Cold War creatures as Senator McCarthy and his hordes of Red-baiters, who were capable of whipping up mass panic and anxiety to levels barely comprehensible to us now.

Nothing proved more alarming, however, than the eruption of the civil rights movement, except the solidarity with the rising demonstrated by many white Southern politicians, churchmen, and ordinary citizens. For my aunt, the effort of blacks and their white comrades against the settled segregationist order of the South was 1865 all over again, with the same dire horsemen of chaos and anguish sure to follow. But if it felt to her like the end of a world, it indeed was one. My aunt's racial prejudices had never before been called into question, hence never been raised, in her mind, to the plane of principled ideology. Segregation was the "way things were," an order of things that comprehended every stratum and nook of Southern society, and made it legible, negotiable. The televised images of civil rights demonstrations and conflicts pulled this contented view of the world to the surface of her mind, stripped it of contentment, and revealed its dissonance with values that, like segregation, she also held to be eternal—the fair play and plain dealing entrenched in all Americans' view of their civilization, and the Christian ideal of human equality before God. As Vandalia might have come eventually to realize—but never acknowledged in fact—her piety, her devotion to the biblical proclamation of liberty and justice put her closer, in terms of essential belief, to Dr. King than to any white racist demagogue.

In the end, however, she did not reject segregationism, the only way of life she had ever known; nor did she embrace any current attempt to dismantle racism's dismal reign. She was not about to enlist as a foot soldier in *defense* of segregation, if only because George Wallace and the brutal Mississippi police she saw on television were white trash, whom my aunt had been raised to abhor. She was thus left with nothing—without unshaken faith in the collapsing structures and values of her high-horizoned, patriarchal world, and without confidence that the new political order, whether segregated or integrated, would allow her to keep her dignity through the changes. So it was that Aunt Vandalia, in common with countless other Southerners of her sort, withdrew into the two remaining consolations open to her in that desperate cultural moment: prayer and genealogy.

To my knowledge, she had never before taken any purposeful interest in family history and bloodlines. Nor had anybody among our immediate kin done so. But abruptly, Vandalia began the research that would eventually find its way to the attic—posting inquiries to relatives ever more distant, answering their letters, then sending messages farther abroad, always to genealogists more or less like herself: older, leisured Southern folk busy with the establishment of respectable ancestries. Because the agenda of this vast genealogical industry was set by the fear of social disorder, miscegenation, and social ruin, it urged on all its participants the construction of an *ideal* family tree. This legacy need not feature a European noble, or royalty; indeed, given royal Europe's famous decadence, hereditary madness, and despotism, a king among one's ancestors could be positively undesirable. Wanted, rather, was a solid lineage of sturdy white Southerners, risen from lowly pioneer stock to admirable position in church, state, and society. Such a genealogy would include, in the greatest profusion possible, yeoman settlers of Virginia, Revolutionary patriots, Civil War heroes on the Confederate side, together with honorable lawyers, gentlemen farmers, and other male upholders of Southern tradition and traditional virtue. Apart from their necessary biological role in propelling the family line into the future, women held little interest for genealogists of my aunt's generation—unless, of course, a fortunate marriage to a lady anchored one's male line back to a President or some other illustri-

ous personage (as such a marriage did for my lower South Carolina
relatives, all kin to Thomas Jefferson). And along with women, accuracy and candor were also matters of minor concern. What counted,
in this work of quietly anxious genealogizing, was a clear bloodline
back to a time before everything began to fall apart.

During the years she spent in this inquiry, Aunt Vandalia's corre-
spondents did very well by the Mays family. Her branch, they
demonstrated to her satisfaction, came from an old and venerable
vine, with roots thrust deeper into American soil than any family not
French, Spanish, or aboriginal. By the end of her archiving of our
dead, Vandalia had accumulated quite enough decent, prosperous
ancestors to enable her to claim long tenure on the Southern soil,
high respectability for her Mays kin, and badges to wear upon her
bosom, as a Daughter of the American Revolution. Not that she'd
ever doubted she could claim such things—though she was most
happy to get written confirmation that her claim to elite Southern
lineage was legitimate.

She was particularly proud to confer upon her kin the rarest gift
of all: discovery of a founding ancestor who had landed on these
shores a full decade before 1620 and the arrival of the *Mayflower*—an
Anglican clergyman already planted on Virginia's soil, that is, when
the radical, meddlesome brood of future Yankees were elsewhere,
and still just trouble in the making. William Mays—the name first
appears in a letter written in 1616 from the famous Jamestown settler John Rolfe to King James I—also had the virtue of being no
indentured servant, no fortune-hunting fop, but a Christian minister
of the Gospel. In 1610, he had sailed from England across the
Atlantic in obedience to the Bishop of London, to serve the twenty
male members of the Virginia Company and their families in the
company's second parish, now at Hampton, on Chesapeake Bay.
From the loins of priest William, all the genealogists in my aunt's
circle of researchers agreed, sprang John, destined to become a
tobacco planter, in 1615. From father William and son John
descended many venerable generations and families, including our
own. The published source universally invoked to prove the Reverend William's descent to the end of the nineteenth century was *A
Partial History of the Mayes Family of Virginia and Kentucky,* printed in a
small edition at Jackson, Mississippi, in 1906. The author's name is

given as "Judge Edward Mayes, Esquire." Its authority was not questioned.

That the discovery of a priest in Jacobean Virginia as our founding patriarch would come as happy news to Aunt Vandalia and her colleagues needs no explanation here. Nor, given what I have already said about my deliberate forgetting of roots, is there any reason to spell out why the assertion bored me upon Aunt Vandalia's revelation of it, during a time of desperate mental disarray, and interested me not at all when, after her death, the printed authority turned up in the attic. If interest in the South had once preoccupied me to paralyzing effect, genealogy had never held the slightest attraction. The only engaging ancestors I had, to my certain knowledge, were clever little hominids who had accomplished much more in the Olduvai gorge two million years ago—the art of fashioning stone choppers, for instance—than any seventeenth-century Englishman ever did in Virginia. What Anglican divine could possibly be more fascinating than the original owners of Dr. Leakey's bones?

But while William Mays failed to cause a surge of family pride in me, Edward Mayes kindled a tiny, quick flicker of curiosity. Sitting on the floor in the attic's dust and stifling heat, riffling through the brittle rot in Aunt Vandalia's carton of ancestral memories, I was beset by a single question. What caused Edward Mayes, whoever he was—indeed, what event would cause *anybody*—to put his hand to the direly laborious task of digging down through records lying three hundred years deep, to gather up the names of ancestors nobody before him had ever thought important enough to locate?

Finding the answer involved a journey that would take me farther than I ever expected to go: out of the twentieth century altogether, into the conflict-ridden aristocratic imagination of the South in the wake of the Civil War and defeat, into the dark waters that roiled at the bottom of my Mays kin's understanding of themselves, and their mission. But the mental travel began simply enough, with a desultory attempt to discover who this "Judge Edward Mayes, Esquire" really was.

It was a short order, as things turned out, since my cousin Edward had been a notable Mississippian—not himself a judge, though the son of one—and had left behind him a considerable trail of biographical evidence. He was born near Jackson in 1846, the last child of a native Virginian and lawyer named Daniel, who had followed the westward-tracking American frontier to Kentucky, taught law and served as a judge there, and, in 1839, moved west the last time, to the young city of Jackson. By the time Daniel and Elizabeth Mayes arrived, the Choctaw had ceded their millions of Mississippi acres to the United States and moved west, and the administrative center of the new American state had been laid out on a rational urban plan, proposed for the site years before by Thomas Jefferson. The capitol building was occupied by the state government the same year Daniel arrived; the railroads were usurping the rivers as arteries of trade. And even as incoming farmers from farther east were erasing the central highland forests of Mississippi, the new industrial and commercial city in the midst of this general destruction was burgeoning. Edward's father saw the opportunities Jackson held out for an ambitious lawyer, and seized them. Upon the outbreak of war in 1861, Edward rushed back from school in Virginia to Jackson, where he clerked in a clothing store until the city's destruction by Union troops in the summer of 1863. Not yet fourteen, he fled the burning capital north to the village of Carrollton, where he found a job teaching school; and, not yet fifteen, he joined the Confederate cavalry, fighting with them until hostilities ceased in Mississippi, on May 6, 1865.

Like countless other Southerners initiated into manhood on the battlefields of the Civil War—my great-grandfather John Matthew Mays was another one—Edward ended his military service to the doomed Confederacy determined never to look back, either in rage or in pity; and again like my great-grandfather, set about making his way as citizens of hierarchical cultures always do: less by accumulating money than by finding a place at court. The town in which he chose to do so was Oxford. Upon his graduation in law from the University of Mississippi in 1869, he married Frances Eliza Lamar and thereby acquired, along with a wife, the powerful patronage of her father, Lucius Quintus Cincinnatus Lamar, postbellum Mississippi's most prominent politician. Lamar's own path had demonstrated the benefits of a wise marriage. In 1847 he had wed the daughter of Augustus B. Longstreet, outstanding Georgia lawyer, brilliant teacher, antebellum president and chancellor of Ole Miss, and author of charming tales that Edgar Allen Poe found hilarious. In thanksgiving for this connection, Edward gave all but one of his seven children *Lamar* as a middle name. But the greater gift was Lamar's to Edward: the specifics of his life's course, the iconography, one might say, of Edward's own self-construction.

Like Lamar before him, Edward became a law professor at Ole Miss, then university chancellor, and, two years later, built the institution's first library. In his academic trajectory, so also in his writings and practice, Edward carried on the traditions of his great in-law's line. Though Lamar had signed Mississippi's Ordinance of Secession and tirelessly supported the Confederacy while it lasted, after the defeat he immediately stepped forward to become the war-wasted region's most eloquent spokesman for national conciliation, plumping for what he called "the greatness and glory of the American Republic" in Congress, later in the cabinet of President Cleveland, and, finally, on the bench of the United States Supreme Court. Lamar also pressed home the New South ideals of industrialization and the rapid expansion of railways. And so, therefore, did Edward, serving railroad companies as counsel, writing on the Southern Pacific railway, working for his father-in-law's progressive Democratic Party. Edward Mayes would be known today to his family only as he was known to Mississippi—a quietly loyal New South acolyte of his more flamboyant father-in-law, an outstanding Oxford lawyer and dignitary—had he gone to his grave with Lamar, in 1893. He did not; and with Lamar's death, Edward's gaze slowly began to turn away from the future toward the immediate and more remote past, and the writing that would bring him to Aunt Vandalia's attention.

The earliest evidence of his change in the 1890s is the book *L. Q. C. Lamar, His Life, Times, and Speeches, 1825–1893*, published in 1896. He was not to be his patron's most famous biographer; that distinction belongs to John F. Kennedy. The value of the book, for me, lies not in what it tells us about Lamar, but in the cultural index it provides to the Southern decade in which it took shape. In the work, the future Oxford educator and American statesman emerges from childhood as a tragic paragon—left fatherless at age nine by his wealthy young parent's suicide, yet rising above this trauma to great national accomplishment despite all. Near Oxford, in the late 1850s, the city-bred Lamar builds his thousand-acre Solitude plantation, and drops back into his ancestral role as rural gentleman, a "Southern farmer of the highest type," as Edward puts it. In the eyes of his disciple, Lamar at antebellum Solitude is a demigod at rest in his Mississippi Arcadia, "surrounded by his slaves, to whom he was at once master, guardian, and friend, loved and petted by his women folk and his children, visited by cultivated and attractive friends."

It's worth noting that this pastel picture in words—reprinted without comment in a recent scholarly biography of Lamar—depicts a scene Edward did not witness. Nor does Edward bother to tell us that the purchase of Solitude plantation by this "Southern farmer of the highest type" was more politic than pastoral. Lamar disliked the countryside, and lived at Solitude only long enough to secure the loyalty of the powerful rural squirearchy in the Oxford vicinity. But Edward's *L. Q. C. Lamar* is not biography in the strict sense. It represents the mobilization of his father-in-law in an argument for what the author thought were the highest public virtues of an antebellum Southern civilization he barely knew: unflinching fidelity to duty, chivalry in battle and humility in defeat, service to the common good and closeness to the land, sobriety in everything. Whether such notions actually shaped the economic and political structures of the antebellum South—or anything other than the rhetoric by which Southerners have always put great store—is a question I leave to the historians. What counts is that Edward believed they did, and fashioned from these ideas the cultural and psychological construction, the perfect political gentleman, whom we meet in *L. Q. C. Lamar.*

But it still might never have occurred to Edward to turn his Lamar biography into a polemical act of sparing and saving were these values not felt to be menaced, which they were. From the end of the Civil War into the 1890s, the banner of the South had been carried by elders like Lamar, and their heirs-apparent, such as Edward—ambitious lawyers and other educated professionals, born to wealth and privilege before the conflict, reduced to penury by it, resurrected in spite of it. They resolved to prevent any further suffering by white Southerners at the hands of Yankee radicals. This they accomplished by their own management of the South's made-in-Dixie industrial and political reconstruction. The loyalty of Mississippi's white populace, formerly vested in such men when they led armies, flowed in the postwar years to the same people, now back in civilian suits. For a while, that is. By the early 1890s the old, established class of leaders, to which L. Q. C. Lamar belonged, was dying off. Standing ready to snatch the reins of power as soon as they dropped from those aristocratic hands were Mississippi's white small-farm folk, who hated blacks, Yankees, dutiful planters, and patrician Southern lawyers indifferently.

When beginning work on *L. Q. C. Lamar*, during the early years of Mississippi populism's ascendance, Edward had grounds to think his work might encourage a reversal of fortunes and steeling of will in the right sort of Southerners. By 1896, when the biography was published, the contest was all but over, and the conquest of Mississippi politics by the nonpatricians all but certain. Rather than launch another exhortation on the order of *L. Q. C. Lamar* at the public—a foredoomed enterprise, under Mississippi's political skies—the aging lawyer took the same turn that Aunt Vandalia, similarly facing the loss of worlds, was to take some sixty years later. Dismayed by the outer world, he voyaged inward, farther down than family tradition or written history could take him, into the archives and as far down the mine of memory as he could go. The result was Edward's *Partial History*.

The book is slight and jotty, as privately devotional as *L. Q. C. Lamar* is openly political; yet, like much devotional writing, it speaks to the longing in us for the richness denied by this fallen world. The work opens with the declaration, based on what evidence nobody knows, that the family of Mayes is probably of Dutch origin. "Certain it is, that in Holland there was a family of some historical celebrity of the name of Maas or Maes . . . even so far back as the year 1476, considered an 'ancient family.'"

And plod though it may from this beginning onward, the author's fast listing of Dutch merchants who "probably" settled in England, and hatched our family's ancestors there, nevertheless sets the tone of the whole book firmly. These forebears were ambitious, successful businessmen and politicians and diplomats, heirs to neither inherited wealth nor title. What money they had, they won by their labor and integrity, not the patronage of kings. Indeed, the prominent European kinsmen in the Maas family, Edward suggests, were Enlightenment men *avant la lettre*. When, in 1555, Charles V renounced his claim over the Netherlands, opening the way for the establishment of the republic, Jacob Maas, "a member of the council of Brabant, a man of great learning, eloquence and prolixity," delivered a memorable speech in praise of the newfound freedom from monarchy. In Jacob, Edward had found a presumed ancestor of exactly the right sort; and the bearing and character of a person of the right sort, according to the Lamarckian assumption underpinning all genealogy, is eminently inheritable. From this Dutch ancestor through the Reverend William of Virginia and all William's American offspring, Edward traces the acquired genes of self-possession, "great learning," and justice, and hence, the right to rule the unruly that was being stripped from his kind of Mississippian.

As I pondered Edward's *Partial History,* its author gradually emerged from the pages as a man wholly of the nineteenth century, though one of a certain type that I recognized—a *Southern* type, in more than one sense. There was his tacit assumption, for example, that genealogy is, or can be, cultural therapy—as distinct from its other familiar uses, such as establishing the heir to a crown, and providing harmless diversion. Edward believed that calling to mind the noble dead of one's family can revive and ennoble the recaller's soul, heal his alienation from the present-day world, and inspire him to imitate the mighty deeds of old; or, as Sister Erin was fond of saying, "to live up to the Mays name." For both Edward Mayes and Sister Erin, the source of this conviction lay in the Classical education both received, and in the Classical precedents suffusing Southern elite culture—especially the precedents afforded by the Romans, who were obsessed with genealogy of this sort. Hence, the shape of Edward's book: no heap of stony facts, piled up prodigiously after the Modern "objective" historiographical fashion of his time, but a gallery of noble portraits, rescued from obscurity.

But underlying the method—and the peculiarly Roman emphasis Southerners like Edward put on the word *genealogy*—is a still more ancient idea, having to do with *time.* As we are told by Mircea Eliade, the great student of myth, the Modern mind since Darwin imagines time to be continuous, unbroken—stretching away from the present into the historical, geological, cosmic past in a straight, unbroken line to infinity. To the pre-Modern sensibility of Livy or Plutarch—to traditional Southern consciousness—time, says Eliade, is "subject to periodical ruptures which divide it into 'secular duration' and a 'sacred time,'" the latter being the better, more heroic and noble. From the "sacred time" of Rome's finest, earliest moment, for instance, the priest and moralist Plutarch drew up his exemplary portraits, in the hope of improving the stunted souls doomed to live in "secular duration."

Ideally, however, the work would go beyond mere improvement to a full restitution of the Golden Age by valiant souls set on fire by the glimpse of primordial glories. But for Edward, as for every conventional moralist, the possibility ever looms that any such attempt at renewal will be overtaken by doom. Close to the end of his book, my cousin inserts a versified apostrophe composed by his father, addressed to the year 1831, after hearing a particularly gloomy sermon in January 1832. It is a work of poesy, I should add, quotable less for its literary merit than for the witness it bears to the pessimistic Southern sentiment about time.

Where now are the hopes that sprang up at thy dawning?
The heart-thrilling joys by fond fancy portrayed,
When we greeted with gladness thy first, fairest morning,
As it rose, in its bright, golden beauty arrayed?
The answer: all hope has fled with the year's ending.
The lamp of thy life—I've beheld its expiring.
Like a dream of the night, thou hast vanished away.
How joyous thine entry! how sad thy retiring!
How short of thy promise, the close of the day!

The second trip to Oxford took place in the summer of 1988. I went there, not to prepare myself to write this book—Aunt Vandalia was still alive, and I had not yet discovered Edward Mayes—but rather at the request of *Destinations*, my newspaper's travel magazine. The editor wanted a story about a small American town. It could be anywhere, as long as there was something unique to see, to *sense* there. Oxford came to mind at once, if only because I had sensed something in the town I never quite understood or resolved in the years following my first visit. This lack of resolution had not exactly haunted me. But it had lain in the bottom of my mind, like the boxes in the attic that Aunt Vandalia always meant to sort out, and did not get to—*wanting* to be sorted out, if not insisting that it be done. So I returned, and discovered something about the South, and about being Southern, that would make sense only after I began to write this still-unimagined book.

When I got there, the square's lines of postbellum storefronts, memorials to the prosperity that began to fade around 1890, were more or less intact. The slender man, memorializing the Confederate dead, was exactly as I had left him years before. But apart from the oldest glass-fronted emporiums, and the soldier and the courthouse, almost everything seemed different. The malls and fast-food franchises, the blight of all the South, had arrived. My hotel on the square was closed, but the once-forbidden Faulkner mansion was open. The population of the square seemed older, quieter. Farmers no longer came up in wagons from their Yocona River lands to trade. The vegetable market had vanished, and Mr. Sneed's hardware store had been replaced by Jenny's Hallmark Cards. At least one excellent store had been added—Square Books, founded and operated by Richard Howorth, son of a distinguished Oxford family—but the elderly men in white shirts, who sat across from it in the shadow of the courthouse, played dominoes no longer.

What struck me as most sharply different was the way I was in Oxford. Or, to put the matter differently, the way the town now seemed to lay itself open to me.

In the early 1960s, partly because of my literary training, partly because of the incomprehensibility of my own thoughts then, I had come to Oxford to seek the South that lay behind, within, the novels and stories of William Faulkner. That was the naïve way literary students thought criticism was, back in those days: excavation, a patient unearthing of the nugget of truth or existential meaning entombed in the brick and mortar of language. But my inclination to read texts in this manner was rooted in a more pervasive conviction, dating back to my first year in the university, when I took an introductory course in Greek philosophy. From that time I had never doubted the truth of the fragment of Heraclitus that tells us that "Nature loves to hide." I imagined Heraclitus' maxim meant that reality was dodging around *beneath something*. The job of intellect, as I understood it, was to dig down through the rubble and uncover the treasure, strip away the wrapping to reveal the truth presumably concealed at the center.

Hence the anxiety that surged inside me the first time I came to Oxford, felt the South of the stone soldier's "fathers' faith" near at hand, but could not plumb the *essence* of the South I felt to be hiding in Oxford.

In that season of troubled searching for ground to stand on, I had read many writers' opinions about the presumed essence of the South. Such opinions are without number. From at least the 1930s, and the publication of *I'll Take My Stand*—the famous agrarian manifesto by twelve writers (including Allen Tate, John Crowe Ransom, Robert Penn Warren) opposed to the industrialization, the *Americanization*, of the South—there had been a huge American industry devoted to thinking up and writing down and printing such notions of essence. (*Mutatis mutandi* it still exists today.) But even when thinking hard about my homeland, as I was during the last season of my drive back to Southern archaism, those opinions about *essence* refused to make sense. The writer I happened to be reading meant by *South* either a heap of regional peculiarities that meant very little to me—grits, magnolias, the Klan, our drawl, and so forth—or some glowing, elusive goodness apparently embedded in an agrarian past that seemed irretrievable.

But I might better have understood that difficulty, and the frustration of my first journey to Oxford, had I ever given serious thought to another haunting fragment of Heraclitus' philosophy, this time a reminder. "We do not notice how opposing forces agree," he says. "Look at the bow and the lyre." No translation I've seen—even this one by the great American writer Guy Davenport—does justice to the saying's luminosity, though its teaching is surely as obvious as anything in everyday life. Living with parallel verities is simply what that life is very largely about. The essential truth about myself, or any text, or *anything*, is not a simple kernel locked away inside a worthless, obfuscating husk, as common sense inclines us to think. Rather, ultimate realities of both life and art are all on the surface: plural and various, conflicting, coinciding. *Truth* is, or should be, a plural noun, denoting shifting ground plans and patterns of reality, iridescent, revealing and disclosing continually. From this it follows that the only worthwhile way of knowledge is *knowing*, as one knows another person, not prying and studying, but joining in the endless mirror-play of options and opposites and changes that consti-

tutes the truth of any lover, friend, or enemy, and that surely consti-
tutes whatever reality we'll ever know. Being alive, or so it seems to
me, is to be continually at variance with oneself, yet no less continually in agreement—to live within contradiction. "Look at the bow
and the lyre."

It was Heraclitus who inclined me on that second visit to stop looking for some essential *South* in Oxford, and drew my mind away to the
harmonic play of differences at work in the very plan of the town
itself. The bow in this paradigm is the commercial square, the lyre is
the academic circle. Laid out a mile from the circle at the other end of
a straight street, the square speaks of sobriety and order, spelled out in
its prosperously appointed stores, law offices, and its central courthouse, with its upsweep of column, jamb, and crisp vertical edge—the
spirit of postbellum Southern optimism and dominion inscribed on
the very ground. The square is replete, complete, *filled.*

The circle, at the heart of the University of Mississippi's oldest
Classical temples, is as empty as the square is full: an open grove of
ancient trees, with nothing under them but quiet. No central spire or
other culminating architectural statement interrupts its emptiness.
The circle's symbolism is deliberate, eloquent—expressing an ideal of
civilization as *agora*, a gathering around a central silence in which
thoughts flow, mingle, disperse.

Its symbolism is no less plainspoken than that of the square,
which proclaims civilization as an imposition of structure, a secular
acropolis from which emanates law and the force of law to the farthest bounds of city, county, world. Taken together, the open field of
the circle, the sturdy monumental courthouse on the square, a clearing and a closing—a bow and lyre—seemed to express the South I
had been looking for, written on the very earth. If I'd come to a dead
end in the 1960s, trying to define the South as a single thing I could
belong to, I now witnessed in Oxford a definition that worked better:
a chord created by the beautiful conflict of the string and the bow
that makes it sing, making music in that very confrontation.

As much as any nineteenth-century American could be, L. Q. C.
Lamar was close to an understanding of the South, and of America,
as a harmony produced by such pluralities. Within his mature life
and thought there resided a conviction about the South, *his* South, as
a certain circulation and tension between ideas, new and old, institu-

Gravesite, Carolina low country

tions obsolete and yet coming to be—Southern civilization, not as an abstract thing, but as a kind of music. It involved living out the tension between America and the South, and with all the ambiguities such paths involve—paths of life that neither Lamar's son-in-law nor many other white, highborn Southerners of Edward's anxious generation were able to live with. So, at the end of his life—as I tried to do at the outset of mine, and Aunt Vandalia did in the midst of her own—Edward chose to idealize the culture of the circle, antique and heroic, Roman and Stoic, and find in the history of his family the Ciceronian examples of manhood and virtue that he believed to be vanishing from contemporary Mississippi humanity.

The latter thoughts came to me a few years after 1988, after I had discovered Lamar, and Edward, and the closeness of my kinsman to Oxford. It was after reading Edward's genealogical book that I decided the next step toward finding my roots in the South—by that time, I was ready—involved *not* following cousin Edward's example, and *choosing* which South is "real." In my distraught early years, I had tried to resolve the tension between myself as *free* and myself as *Southern* by extinguishing the second term of the opposition. I imagined a stern, soul-wrenching choice had to be made, between the South and America, ruralism and modernity, the constriction of long history on the land and the groundless liberties of the city. Edward's strategy was, similarly, to eliminate existence's troublesome freedom and alienation by imagining himself a hapless, old-fashioned product of a noble family history rolling forward with unbroken momentum through centuries. The beauty of Southern culture—the beauty calling to me from history and the ground, issuing its gentle invitation to rethink once more my Southern origins—arose in the very conflicts and contrasts of the versions of *South* that have been created on this land by my family, and thousands of other families, during the centuries of our fragile tenure on it.

It was on Oxford's circle one soft, warm evening during my third visit to Oxford, after Aunt Vandalia's death—now thinking of Edward and his university library just opposite, again sensing the South close at hand, though no longer terrifying—that these thoughts began to come gently toward me.

During such twilights, there is no place in Oxford more beautiful than the grove at the university's heart. The heat of late afternoon seems to end abruptly, just as the sun sinks behind the trees beyond the Lyceum, and the evening breeze springs up, high in the branches. As darkness gathers under them, the trees become great columns holding up green lintels, and the air in that temple is suffused with golden light. High in the treetops, the birds begin their evening songs, and near the ground, the fireflies come out, a scatter of pulsing embers across the lawn. In that dusk, ancestral spirits seemed to rise with the mists beneath the trees, not to devour but to remind, and summon up mindful recollection. These long-dead Southern kinsmen brought histories of mastery over land and arms, and defeat by them, tales of the violence endured and inflicted, that are as much parts of being Southern as wise dialogue with earth and weather, Xenophon and Virgil, upcountry barbarism and mechanical industry.

The spirits asked for neither obedience nor imitation; only that I hear the music of bow and lyre. So I listened to what the spirits sang, and wrote.

2

BOOKS OF GENESIS

Marker, James River

"*TELL ME ABOUT THE SOUTH,*" ASKS THE YOUNG CANADIAN Shreve McCannon of Quentin Compson, his Mississippi roommate at Harvard, in *Absalom, Absalom!* "*What's it like there. What do they do there. Why do they live there. Why do they live at all.*" These famous uncomprehending questions toward the end of Faulkner's tragedy of dynasties—or, rather, blunt statements demanding simple replies that would be absurd or trivial, like all declarations about the "essence" of something—came back to me while I was fecklessly sorting out and sifting Aunt Vandalia's papers and other possessions in Greenwood, many years after reading Faulkner's novel.

What do they do there. Nothing much sprang to mind. A few white Southerners, in a brief moment in time, had executed a body of powerful writing. A larger number of black Southerners, over a much longer time, had created blues and jazz. But as for *doing things,* at least as Shreve McCannon understood them, in his bottom-line, Gradgrindian sense—I could think of nothing. Southerners have never *done* things, it seemed to me—at least not in any way that's very original. We have always just *been* there; and if we had perfected anything, they were the traditional arts of being there: good conversation and manners, and knowing how to belong effectively to the conventional communities of church and town. Such remained the South's chief legacy to the world, even more eminent than portable products like books or jazz, though surely less wanted than either.

Why do they live there. Or to rephrase the question as it came to me: *What does it mean to live, to be there, and to think forever of oneself as someone who belongs there?* To do so, of course, was to summon up recollections of the painful breaks that had disrupted that belonging. But, by 1990, these were far enough behind me to allow the long-shut temple doors of the past to swing open, and the Muse, solemn Mnemosyne, to speak from her sanctuary deep in time. Recalled to what I had been in earliest childhood, and to a way of boyhood and plantation life that had changed little since the nineteenth century, I found that world warm and clear, and full of hints as to *why we live there*, and why the South still lives on even in those of us who've left it. For me the first firm memory to form in that golden mist had to do with the courtesy of living and being on Southern earth, the assurances preserved in stories passed within our families and communities, and down bloodlines from generation to generation.

Tell me about the South. What's it like there. On a certain autumn afternoon in my childhood, it was like this.

The green rows of cotton plants, picked neat of white bolls now, fell away west from my father's house, rolling over the day-warmed hills until they disappeared into sunset's cool haze on the horizon. Supper came, corn and black-eyed peas and ham, and after that I waited, restless, for the sun to sink a little farther behind the trees, then for the moonrise that let the hayride start. Of that autumn journey down into the desolate bottomland east of the house, in the direction of the Red River, I remember the swish and swish of sweet hay forked onto the wagon before we set out, the whispers of my sisters and their teenaged friends on the chilly air, the stamping of mules ready to pull—the abrupt complaint of board grinding on iron when the wagon heaved forward from the barn's driveway onto the paved road, and again when it bumped off the road onto the dirt track that led across the pastures into the deeps of the swampy bottom.

The open fields of cotton plants, gilded by harvest moonlight, were soon behind us, and the dank murk under shrubs and trees began to crowd close against the narrow trace the wagon clattered along, now only a moonlit crevice in the thick, high gloom. Then the narrow track opened a little, broadening at last into the tangled front garden of the Big House; and we had arrived.

The deserted plantation house, its lofty and once-pale columns of plastered brick grayed off by time, windows blank and black, stood under the trees in moon shadow beyond a derelict garden. The dance of light from the bonfire on the tall façade seemed to give the house a weird, unreal liveliness. Nobody would have dared go in it, or even close to it because, of course, it was haunted. Though we knew the Big House had been there forever—or at least since that remote era the storytellers designated the Old Time—its origin, its builder and owner, were all unknown. So instead of history, the Big

House breathed stories into the enchanted air around the bonfire, which were caught by the tellers, and told.

Time was when bandits roamed the densely forested, wet delta of the Red, preying on settlers making their way upcountry along boggy ox tracks from the river city of Shreveport to new farms in Texas. Somewhere deep in the lowland bush was a big rock, strange in this alluvial terrain, under which the bandits hid the gold and silver they had looted from the bodies and wagons of their victims, thereby amassing a great treasure.

They were destined never to enjoy the cache, however. For at the call of migrants fearful for their lives and property, armed lawmen arrived from downriver, stalking the Louisiana bottomland until they surprised and captured the notorious thieves and murderers. Even in the face of certain execution, the bandits would not disclose the location of the rock; and as they stood on the gallows, ready for hanging, their leader proclaimed his curse: that he who found the rock, and dared dig for the hoard beneath it, would surely die.

Years passed, and though many a boy and man searched for it in the trackless bottom, no one found the rock. Until, that is, the afternoon the two sons of the Big House, hunting deer and rabbits in the bottom, happened upon a strange and moss-bearded stone, half-hidden under snaking vines. Having heard rumors of the treasure, but conveniently, foolishly forgetting the curse laid on it, the delighted lads set to work at once, clawing away at the soft clay under the rock until their busy fingers tore into a rotted bag, and the loot lay gleaming in the forest's scattered light. The boys returned to the Big House at once, intending to round up some farmhands to help excavate and haul out their treasure trove. But they had no sooner reached the edge of the front garden than a terrible sickness took hold of them, and both died in sweats and agony that very night. Rejecting the consolations of religion and the finalities of Christian burial, the master and his wife, deranged by grief, had two graves dug by lantern light before dawn, and buried their only offspring at the edge of the garden. They never admitted visitors or left the Big House again, staying in the shuttered darkness until their neighbors gradually forgot them. Shrouded in that forgetfulness, they died, or left by night for parts unknown. And from their time to now, no one had ever dared set foot in the Big House.

On certain evenings during the harvest moon, the story went, the shades of the planter and wife, glowing like foxfire, make their mournful way across the weedy grounds of the Big House, weeping for the sons who, in their greed for unearned gain, recklessly disregarded the old warning, and paid the most bitter price.

Listen! the teller would say. *Can you hear them coming?*

Already huddled around the bonfire against the damp chill lying low in the garden before the Big House, we huddled together even closer, and listened intently. And if I heard no slow, rustling footsteps in the brittle grass that autumn night, and saw no ghostly figures mourning their dead sons, I understood, in the way children understand such things, the message of the tale well enough. It had to do, for one thing, with presumptuous forgetfulness; and with the difference between the dark bottomland, with its mysteries and dangers, and the sunny, inhabited upland, kept open to the sun by human work and dwelling. In the end, however, the lesson was about the people we should be, *must* be: careful walkers in the light of Mnemosyne's lamp, folks who remember the old warnings, and heed them.

When a child, of course, I understood none of the weightier implications of the ghost story told at the bonfire before the Big House. They came to mind as I sat at Aunt Vandalia's desk that warm night after she died, along with a deepening ache and sense of irrefragable loss. I had left the South, in part, to lose the ancient tales that bind the soul against the snatching and loosing of Modern times, but also cast every Southern soul into a type within the range of Southern moral portraiture.

Sister Erin, for instance, born in Alabama in 1881 during the postbellum cotton boom, coming of age wealthy at the turn of our century in the east Texas town of Palestine, had learned early what a white, Methodist matriarch-in-training was supposed to be in a culture saturated with normative stories about just that. It meant being musical; so, as part of her "cultivation," as she called it, Sister Erin was packed off to the Cincinnati Conservatory of Music to study voice and piano, and later installed a fine wind-up Victrola and a cabinet of operatic recordings in her house in Greenwood. It meant being pious in both private and public. When in Cincinnati, she once bought a chocolate bar on Sunday, but became so pained by shame at having done so, she dropped the uneaten candy into the garbage—thereby creating an *exemplum* of virtue that she often told, and that became part of the standard curriculum of correct behavior in our family. Her formation instilled in her a conviction that duty is the supreme task of life, not the exercise or expansion of rights—the duty to maintain the balances of privilege and deference in her household, as an example to her community, and to keep firm and stainless the civic image of her family. To my knowledge, she never did what she wanted without reference to the unwritten book of Southern deportment she'd learned by heart as a girl. But because she believed the book to be true, she performed her duties gracefully, never giving the slightest impression of constriction or discomfort in that performance. Essie De, who accompanied me on every child-hood visit up from my father's plantation to Greenwood, remembers Sister Erin's house as strict, with a designated place for everything and everyone. Because Essie De was black, she had to endure lectures by Sister Erin's servants about where she could go and what she could touch. So did I; my earliest lessons in decorum came from Peggy, my grandmother's black cook, who let me know where in the house I could and could not go. Sister Erin never spoke of such matters. She had mastered, that is, the essential prerequisite for making hierarchy work, which is keeping it invisible.

Tell me about the South. Why do they live there. Why do they live at all. I heard the old questions again, but also found that I was asking them of myself; for what I had voluntarily lost I now wanted to find again. What was here, inside me and in Aunt Vandalia's room, that could give me answers? Hundreds of photographs depicting the known of my family, the unknown from another century, and still others I could just remember, men leaning against the porch of my father's house at Spring Ridge and ladies in crisp white dresses, hatted and gloved. There were the photos and diaries and old wills and legal documents pen-scratched in antique hands or, in the case of more recent ones, typed; heaps of letters from relatives and friends saved by Aunt Vandalia and Sister Erin and others for over a century. From these many jagged shards of fact, I could make little sense, and surely not stitch together any coherent knowledge. When I had left the South, I had left behind and lost the key to reassembling the smashed vessel on which the names and identities of my family had been inscribed, and thus found these fragments of text as barely intelligible as Etruscan.

But as I was discovering, I did remember some stories from child-hood, and they were giving a certain order to my need to know where I came from, and from what memories and land. And Aunt Vandalia, as it happened, had gathered up other stories during her stint as a genealogist. The litter of genealogical papers, and tales in my head, and unforgotten public narratives of Southern civilization, its chivalrous, agrarian past and destruction and resurrection, the community of souls extinguished in the Civil War and postwar Reconstruction—all these things seemed to ignite in the forest clear-ing at the edge of trackless dark, like the bonfire at the Big House; and I was again huddled near the fire, hearing narratives of South-ern identity, and the identity of my Southern family, unheard for a long time.

Among the stories in Aunt Vandalia's genealogical papers was, of course, the one laid out in Edward Mayes's genealogical book, which I've described, and to which I'll have reason to return. But I found another account of our Southern family's beginnings, more casual than that written by our cousin Edward, though driven by similar motives: to establish our rootedness in clefts in the rock of deep time, under the shifting sand of the present, perilous moment. For Jewell Mayes, our Missouri relation who jotted down this version in 1931, the force ungrounding everything was the Great Depression. But Jewell's narrative, at first glance, seemed to come from an older spot than Edward's, more laden with richness of mythic, literary orna-ment, and as naked as any folk tales of the historical apparatus by which my Mississippi relation sought to lend his project scholarly ballast. And though I had never before seen this printed legend, it was immediately familiar. For one hot summer's afternoon on the side verandah in Greenwood, before I was ten, Aunt Vandalia had told me the story, or a version of it, over lemonade after Bible study.

In her version, three valiant Mays brothers—Jewell adds a fourth—set sail from Britain many years before the Revolution, their destination the New World, their goal prosperity and freedom. One went to New England, another to Virginia, and still another made landfall in South Carolina. (Jewell's fourth sailor came ashore in

Nova Scotia.) Each was a descendant of a remarkable patriarch, from whose loins we Mayses all sprang.

This Mays—*the* Mays, the archetype and ancestor of us all—was born *Maes* in the Low Countries, and joined the following of William the Conqueror. After the Norman capture of Ireland, he ended up there as *O'Maithe*, ensconced, in Jewell's words, in a "baronial hall on a wee island off the upper east coast." Thus planted in Ireland and enriched through service to the Conqueror, this Baron O'Maithe fathered the first generation of a tribe destined for a reputation of ferocious independence. The Norman-Irish offspring of the patriarch were never again true King's men, and would combine in "an uprising against the Crown centuries later, banishment, and hate for Britain's flag." This anecdote makes out our medieval Mays ancestors as a bloody-minded lot, though, of course, their only importance in the story is to evince the ancient loyalty of the Mays clan to that Southern (and Roman, and Jeffersonian) institution, aristocratic republicanism. Jacob Maas, the valiant sixteenth-century burgher of Brabant, had been mobilized by Edward Mayes to suggest the same high heritage of the Mays descendants. What counts powerfully, and drives the stories, of course, is the establishment of a fixed link, represented by the band of brothers, between the old Mays families of America and a primordial ancestor who lived in the high, remote past. Aunt Vandalia was certain, by the way, that we'd never been anything other than a family anchored by noble virtues in our service to the common man—though the writings of Jewell and Edward, and the mixed version she'd received from our east Texas relations, came as welcome confirmation of the deep rightness of our family's allegiance to Franklin Delano Roosevelt, who came as near to the Southern ideal of the patrician-democrat as any Yankee could hope to.

Reading over this familiar narrative, I found myself pondering the *voices* in Jewell's story, all of them distant yet within reach—echoing up from the darkness down time's well, but not very deep in it, and oddly familiar. The story was almost certainly first formulated during the early years of the American Republic. Throughout the nearly two centuries of American monarchy, after all, most English settlers on the eastern seaboard knew where they came from, and thus had no need of a founding legend, or at least one of heroic and epic shape.

The broadening families of English newcomers, I'd learned in school, tended to stay close to the Atlantic seaboard, and close together, until pushed toward the frontier by shortage of land. But as Edward Mayes suggests, this push of settlement west and south in the seventeenth century quickly led to the separation of Mays relations throughout the South, who lost touch with, and knowledge of, each other.

By the early years of the republic, however, these families would certainly have become aware that other people with the same name existed. Trade and travel, education, and the propagation of American unity encouraged contact. So it was that, in the second or third decade of the nineteenth century, the Mayses of southside Virginia and those of Botetourt County, in the northern part of the Revolutionary commonwealth, and those living in Pennsylvania had encountered one another, and wondered where we came from, and what our connections may have been. The answer, at least among us southside Virginians, appears to have been the legend of the three or four brothers, which explains everything while proving nothing, and inflates the temporary loss of contact among Mays descendants into a great historical project of liberty, hatched by the primordial brothers in the Old Country before their sally forth to the New. The tradition Jewell relates is thus a quintessential expression of genealogical imagination, which—in opposition to Modern historiographical method—always sees connections in coincidences.

What engaged me in Jewell Mayes's account more than its colorful description of our origins, however, was its inner architecture of myth. Or, to be more accurate, how the creator of Jewell's story used one of the most ancient narrative patterns by which the Indo-European families and nations have traditionally explained how we got here, and who we are.

What's interesting is that the creator of this family did not use the more famous pattern, brilliantly embodied in Virgil's *Aeneid*. If Aeneas has been largely forgotten in the populace at large, and hardly anybody reads Virgil's poetry anymore just for fun, his epic still stands at the fountainhead of the rhetoric that continues to roll through patriotic, democratic explanations of how America became glorious, despite its foundation by ragtag immigrants. In Virgil's work of poetic civics, the warrior Aeneas saves himself from calamity, ruin, and disgrace by flight from his doomed city of Troy, eventually making landfall in Italy and founding there a sturdy nation of farmers destined by the gods and their own courage to dominate the world. Virgil wrote the *Aeneid* to give a grand dynastic family tree to the emperor Augustus, who thought he needed one; the eighteenth-century Enlightenment aristocrats who created the idea of the United States thought they needed the same thing, and found in Virgil the model they needed.

To this day, the celebration of Thanksgiving Day, with its recollections of Puritans recently escaped from persecution, and of blessing in the wilderness after oppression in civilized England, remains the great festival of the typical American citizen: the refugee, the exile now come to the victorious end of his arduous *Aeneid*. Thanksgiving Day is, of course, observed throughout the United States—though it would be interesting to know whether a majority of white Americans fits its vision of citizenship. Many North Americans of Spanish descent descend from privileged colonists who were settling on our continent's shores a century before 1620, and the landing of the Roundheads at Plymouth Rock. Only a portion of British descendants in America can really identify with the myth of the *Mayflower*. Southerners who come from old families certainly cannot.

The interest for me in this tale lies not in what it tells us of my family's roots in deep time—there is little here that's even remotely reliable—but in its use of the *other* august myth of family and tribal origin European peoples have inherited from the past. This one celebrated dynasty over individualism, which perhaps explains why it was rejected by the official mythmakers of the early American Republic, and also why it appealed to the unknown, Classically educated antebellum Southerner who made up the story Aunt Vandalia told me.

The story is Greek, not Roman, in origin, and was apparently designed in high antiquity to explain to the boundlessly curious Greeks how they happened to be divided into distinct nations who all spoke the same language. According to this legend, the dispersed commonwealth of the Hellenes—as Greeks called themselves in antiquity, and call themselves now—descended from a man named Hellen, son of Deucalion, the Greek Noah. This Hellen had three sons, each of whom fathered a distinct family, which in turn became one of the principal Greek tribes, Dorian or Ionian or Aeolian.

Throughout the otherwise complex history of their astonishing civilization, the ancient Hellenes never abandoned or elaborated on this simple genealogical tale. It suited them, for perhaps the same reasons it suited my unknown kinsman: its emphasis on continuity with highest antiquity, the underpinning it gave to the notion that Hellenic civilization resulted from an unbroken unfolding in time, that satisfactorily justified their condescension toward those they called barbarians, *barbaroi,* literally, "the incomprehensibles"—everybody, that is, who wasn't Greek. It was also a tale that fits the picture of what the Hellenes know themselves to be: adventurers and invaders, not refugees—which in turn helps explain its allure to Southerners not quite comfortable with the Virgilian myth.

For even Southern folk who don't think about genealogy, and most don't, have a general understanding that the earliest of us came to North America, not as ideological refugees like the pious Puritans, but as economic opportunists dispatched with grants of land to claim America for Crown and empire. Long before the Civil War, the old Southern establishment felt *different* from the newer and vivaciously ambitious citizens of the United States—loyal to the government in Washington, though ever less so as the decades rolled on toward 1861; antimonarchist, to be sure, though increasingly inclined to cherish the continuities with old England, and to idealize the aristocratic ruralism that typified, at least in Southern imagination, the mother country. The fabric of Jewell Mayes's narrative about the Mayses is saturated with such antebellum Southern idealism, and it asserts a right to ascendance, inherited from the baronial O'Maithe, over the less blue-blooded among us—unnamed in the story as I heard it, but surely meaning blacks, new immigrants, rednecks, white trash, Yankees, and other rabble. If O'Maithe's descendants were much given to "hate for Britain's flag," they also cherished British traditions of deference, feudal clan loyalties, and inherited power. And so should we Mays offspring—or so Aunt Vandalia believed when she passed on this Walter Scott-ish tale over lemonade on the side porch in Greenwood after Bible study.

(Speaking of Greeks: the author of Jewell's story knew his Homer. Jewell repeats a durable tradition in our family having to do with a certain Helen Mayes, date and place unknown. This gentle-woman, like her more famous namesake, disappeared into the terri-tory of a heroic enemy—Shawnee this time, not Trojan—whose town was ultimately destroyed, like Troy, by Helen's aggrieved kins-men. It's yet another example of something that might actually have happened, only to be absorbed by the Classical myths in the heads of my ancestors, then finally reemerging as "a truth worth telling"—a warning against strangers, a celebration of Mays heroism, passed along down the unceasing slide of family memory.)

There are few good stories. And my relations told good ones—of the Civil War, of the comings and goings of the Southern families whose blood is mingled in us, stories of the living, stories of the dead. But perhaps all the best tales told in the West, from Homer and Virgil through Tolstoy, Joyce, and Faulkner have always been recited about only a handful of matters—war, the voyage out and home, geneal-ogy. But by the time my first Mays ancestors came to the New World, in the early seventeenth century, the children of the West had tired of having just stories and were demanding truth as well. And from that demand eventually came history, as the concrete study we know now. And it was respect for such history—a respect at one remove, for if Edward Mayes was Modern, he was also South-ern, with a mind ever drawn into past worlds by Classical myth and epic—that gave my Mississippi cousin his determination to establish an improving lesson about his family on slabs of fact.

Until I took his book from Aunt Vandalia's desk, carried it out to the verandah rich in memories of story, and began to read, however, I imagined his *Partial History* to be more matter-of-fact than mythical. Such had been my impression on first reading it. But when I opened the book to the most certain-seeming passages, about Reverend William Mays of Virginia, I began to sense the presence of old and glowing pictures under the surface of his pedestrian prose.

Edward's sketch of our first American ancestor begins with the chartering of the Virginia Company of London by King James I of England and VI of Scotland on April 10, 1606. The joint stock enter-prise was a radiantly ambitious one, intended to ensure England's free access to furs, wine, silk, naval stores, and other commodities otherwise hard to be sure of, because of the meddling of competitive

Old World powers. In the spring of 1607 the first colonizing expedition of 105 men set sail for the wild coast of North America, and were immediately destroyed by disease, starvation, and the depredations of native folk reluctant to share their land with the English newcomers. Another shipment of settlers, after arriving in 1608, met much the same fate as the first, even though company leader John Smith abandoned the doomed attempts to found a winery and silk manufacture, and decided to put in subsistence good crops of the sort grown by their native Algonkian neighbors. Even that failed.

Looked at one way, the Virginia Company's earliest exploits and disasters seem darkly comical, like some crank attempt to grow potatoes in the tundra. The knowledge of New World climatic conditions was not, after all, *that* primitive. Edward, however, deploys his evidence of the earliest days in a dark tableau of doom—to prepare us, it seems, for the sun's imminent break through the inaugural clouds, between 1609 and 1611. In those years came Sir Thomas Dale, justice of the peace, "bearing a code of extraordinary laws"; Sir Thomas Gates, the company's first Virginia deputy, with three hundred fresh settlers in tow; and "William Mease, our ancestor, who went out as a minister of the gospel of the Established church, being then 37 years of age." (*Mease* was one of the several spellings this clergyman used when signing the legal documents that have survived. Edward gives no evidence for William's age, or for the date of his passage to Virginia.)

In Edward's tale, which was turning into a myth of foundation before my eyes, the three prominent men in the Virginia Company embody three fundamental elements of civilization: *law*, in the person of Sir Thomas Dale; the encouragement of *prosperity*, in Sir Thomas Gates and his flock of settlers; and *priestly intercession* between the immortal gods and frail children of men, in the Reverend Mr. Mays. These harbingers of accomplishment arrive from the distant seat of Empire, step ashore, and lo! the divinities cease their thundering against this English intrusion upon their virgin paradise, and smile. "The colony in Virginia began to expand," after years of starving and reduction, says Edward. "New settlements were made at Dutch Gap, Henrico, and Bermuda Hundred: individual grants of property began to be made, and many signs of prosperity appeared."

It is during this admiring recollection of the company's first Golden Age—which dawned with the first successful crops of tobacco—that Edward cites the earliest documentary evidence we have for the existence and work of William Mays or Mease or spell it as you will: the 1616 letter, which I've mentioned earlier, written in England by John Rolfe to King James I. The notice comes during a description of the company's affairs and lands in which Rolfe mentions an outpost called Kecoughtan, at the mouth of the James River some thirty-seven miles below the enterprise's headquarters at James Towne. The wilderness village claimed twenty souls, including one "Capten George Webb," and "Mr. Wm. Mays minister." "It is a pleasant thing to know that our first American," adds Edward, "was self-devoted to so noble a calling, and followed it under circumstances which argue so much of piety and disinterestedness." The location of William's tiny parish is given, accurately, as present-day Hampton, Virginia. Each year, increasing numbers of "apprentices, unmarried women and neat cattle" came out to settle in this earthly paradise of four jurisdictions—James City, Elizabeth City, Charles City, and Henrico City—each "administered with a degree of energy, unselfishness and statesmanlike wisdom perhaps unparalleled in the history of corporations."

But it was precisely this prosperity and peace, abounding on ground once blighted by strife and want, that would become the company's downfall. The King's ministers across the sea turned greedy, and plotted a grand grab of the treasures created by the similarly independent entrepreneurs in Virginia. What they needed was an excuse to act. And they got it, Edward reports, on March 22, 1622, when "the savages, as usual, came unarmed into the houses of the planters, with fruits, fish, turkeys and venison to sell"—then abruptly fell on the colonists, murdering 347 men, women, and children before the slaughter was stopped by company militia. Most settlers then present in Virginia survived the uprising, however, and the tragic episode might have been merely a glitch in the company's expanding fortunes—had not "the court of James I, jealous of the growing power of the Virginia company and of its too republican spirit, seized on the occasion of this massacre to attribute all the calamities of the colony to its mismanagement and neglect, and thus to frame a pretext for dissolving the charter."

It was from this conflict between company and Crown, and during the hearings initiated in London as a result, that the amplest notices of William Mays emerge. In resistance to "the high-handed proceedings of the king and his officers," says Edward, a number of colonists sailed to London to give testimony on behalf of the company's position. "Amongst this number was William Mease, an abstract of whose evidence, favorable to the company's management, is still extant."

His pluck did nothing to stop the King's minions. In 1624 the Crown revoked the company's charter, placed the settlement's administration in the hands of civil authorities, and told the colonists to get on with growing excellent tobacco for the export market. This designation of Virginia as a Crown colony Edward regards an action "in substance a confiscation, effected by tyranny." Following the defeat of his party's suit, Edward writes, William Mays came back to Virginia—"exactly when he returned is not known"—and settled at Newtowne, dying about 1650 at Henrico City.

In the genealogical scheme of things, John Maies (c. 1636–1713), the Reverend William's son, is a character immediately more *historical* in the Modern sense. On April 29, 1668, as Edward discovered in documents of deed and patent, John staked his claim to 293 acres on the south bank of the Appomattox. Or restaked it: the acreage had certainly belonged to him before 1668, by purchase or grant or inheritance. He may have owned more land in this vicinity, and did eventually possess more by the start of the next century. The site lies about two miles upstream from the river's confluence with the James, between the present-day cities of Hopewell and Petersburg. A 125-acre portion of this land was previously granted to one "Ed. Townstall"—the man himself spelled his name *Tunstall*—who then sold the section to "Wm. Maies, father to sd. Jno. Maies."

Reading the patent now, one can almost hear the sigh Edward Mayes breathed when finding it: *Quod est demonstrandum!* A son of the patriarch William had been discovered, excellent in character—a substantial landowner, that is—and agreeable to genealogical imagination in every respect. John was early, and a native-born Virginian; that he was a planter at the mouth of the Appomattox made him slightly less grand than the great self-made squires of the Charles River plantations a few miles east and downriver, but still a man firmly woven into the first imperial outpost of English civilization to be established in what is now the United States. He had satisfactorily mapped the river of honorable blood, flowing with power from primordial, antityrannical Virginia to him and his elite family of lawyers and statesmen, entrepreneurs and patriots and planters in the troubled South at the turn of this century.

Whether Edward did die peacefully, I cannot say. But he will never rest quietly in the earth of Mississippi, as long as my cousin Joseph Barron Chandler, Jr., is alive and busy. A lawyer in Raleigh, North Carolina, for many years an unflagging student of Mays family history, this brilliant analyst of colonial legal documents says that, if Edward Mayes practiced law as he did genealogy, he would have been disbarred. In his exhaustive studies of the extant proofs for John Maies and William Mays, Joe Chandler has found nothing to support Edward's claim that William was thirty-seven when he disembarked at the Virginia Company's settlement, though the priest did make landfall almost certainly in 1609 (not 1611, as Edward says). In his account of William's later years, Edward states that William came back to the Virginia community of Newtowne after his failed mission to London. Where he got this idea is anybody's guess. Moreover, as Joe has written sternly, "the claim that he lived in Newtowne is demonstrably wrong, a fact which could have been discovered by competent court house research *at the time* [*the* Partial History] *was written*." Edward merely glanced at secondary publications about Newtowne, and found the name *William* there; "and, since it suited his needs, he didn't check the deed records." Nor, Joe believes, is there any unassailable evidence to show that "Wm. Maies, father to sd. Jno. Maies" was the Reverend William Mays mentioned in John Rolfe's letter to King James.

But though surrounded by the debris left on the ground after his masterful assault on Mays genealogy's most sacred belief—the unbroken line back from us to the Reverend William Mays of Virginia—Joe Chandler has always ended his discussions with a firm refusal to lop William off the root of our American family tree. Absolute proof is absent, but the mass of circumstantial evidence Joe has accumulated from seventeenth-century documents strongly suggests the descent of John Maies, as son or (probably) grandson, from Reverend William; and everything indicates our own descent from John.

In addition, the rarity of the name *Mays* in the first years of Virginia, both as company and colony, and the improbability of two unrelated men named William Mays living in Virginia at the right time and the right place, all point toward this clergyman as the ancestor of us all.

Whatever his disagreements and reservations, however, Joe would agree with Edward Mayes and Aunt Vandalia, and with other chroniclers of the Mays families of America, that the Reverend William Mays would make an interesting relation in any family tree.

William was born, perhaps in Cambridgeshire, in the middle of Elizabeth's reign, when the religious strife that had wracked Christianity in England for most of the post-Reformation sixteenth century was in a lull. It was also a moment in which Anglicanism was nearing the stable definition that strife had long prevented: Catholic in teaching and order, but not Roman; Reformed, but neither Calvinist nor Lutheran. Even as this new, and peculiarly English, understanding of what it means to be Christian was becoming customary, in the countryside as well as at court, a significant body of opinion in the Church remained faithful to Calvinism's more radical ideas of reformation. It was from this tendency that Puritanism would arise, to defy and temporarily defeat mainstream Anglicanism, until it was itself extinguished at the Restoration.

Long before Oliver Cromwell's rebellion, however, the Puritan clergy were men to be reckoned with. And it seems almost certain that William Mays was shipped overseas in 1609, along with other Jacobean clergy of the Church of England whose political and religious inclinations are more definitely known, because of his Calvinist and Puritan, hence deeply suspect, beliefs about ecclesiastical polity and doctrine. Be that as it may, it is improbable that any Church of England clergyman would have gone happily and voluntarily to Virginia, for at the time of William's arrival, the outpost was beset by economic and human disaster.

The company's New World enterprise must have seemed doomed to failure in 1609, and would certainly have met that fate, had it not been for an event that would radically alter the fortunes of Virginia, and English America. It was John Rolfe's first successful harvest, in 1614 at Varina Plantation, on the James River, of tobacco grown from seeds imported from Varinas, Spain. What native American tobacco had been previously grown by the settlers was uneconomically bitter; leaf from the new strain was immediately more desirable back in the home market. (The Christian name of Jefferson Davis's wife, incidentally, was Varina—a name, but also a theological title, resonating in the minds of the Rebel planters of 1860 with thoughts of the seed that had brought the South its earliest abundance, and the wealth necessary for independence; a Mother of the Nation indeed.) Shortly after the harvest, Rolfe married Pocahantas—not to satisfy "carnall affection, but for the good of this plantation, for the honor of our countrie." While these sentiments fall on modern ears with a prudish clang, they speak of a commitment to land and homeland, and an understanding of life as service to the common good, that would seem deeply *right* to Southerners for centuries after Rolfe brought in the first, momentous Varina harvest.

For William, a career begun under conditions of great hardship suddenly turned to blessing; and Virginia's newfound prosperity, to his Calvinist imagination, must have seemed a visible sign of Divine Providence, now smiling on the enterprising planters he served. At some time before the dissolving of the company in 1624, he acquired membership in it—a valuable possession, entailing a grant of land that was usually obtainable by investment, though, in his case, was probably given as a reward for his notable service to the corporation. William felt strongly enough about ensuring its continued existence that he sailed to England during the final stages of the controversy over the company's future and became the first signator of an affidavit opposing the dissolution. He was certainly defending his land, but he was also espousing opinions we would expect of a Puritan clergyman: *for* prosperous business interests, *against* the Crown— especially when the crown happened to rest on the brow of dissolute, autocratic James I.

Whether William returned to Virginia after 1624 is not known. The witnesses Joe Chandler has unearthed suggest he did not. A man named William Mays or Maies did own land in England's Virginia territory following the company's disbanding—perhaps farmer, perhaps absentee landlord—and he did have at least one son, our ancestor John. A genealogist of the Mays families need not first smudge his soul with wishful thinking to declare that this William was himself the son of the Anglican clergyman who came ashore in 1609, hence the link in time and blood between me, Joe, and myriad other living Mays kinfolks, and the foundational event in the history of English America. All that's lacking to prove forever these statements is a meeting of the numerous lines of evidence that insistently draw the eye toward a focus of kinship—lines that, so far, have not quite touched.

But what difference does it make? Why should it make a difference at all, if this convergence of hints should ever take place, or whether any of us now living will persist long enough to see it?

When I was first going through Aunt Vandalia's genealogical files, still grieving for the kinswoman I had so recently buried, the only curiosity I was concerned to understand was that of Edward Mayes. But in trying to come to grips with that interest, I would eventually encounter others, more rigorously concerned about the facts of our family's history that cousin Edward ever was. And it was during the earliest exchanges of letters with those inquiring kin that the questions began to seethe again in my mind. What lies behind the determination of Joe Chandler, a proudly liberal Southerner enjoying a full professional life in high appointive office with the North Carolina government, to spend many hours throughout his entire adult life ferreting out new documents of his family, and subjecting both new and familiar ones to careful exegesis and interpretation, all with no financial or other tangible end in view? What longing made my cousin Steven Griffin Mays, a Dallas computer engineer, forever roam the dim, weedy field of the past—its overgrown paths crowded by books, courthouses, and tombstones—gathering up the dried flowers of anecdote, legend, inscription? And, for that matter, what long-dormant inclination was alerted in me when I sat on the verandah, puzzling over Edward Mayes's speculations on the elusive Anglican divine that may, or may not, stand at the head of our American lineage?

The deepest motivations behind these diverse awakenings to the past—which seem to light up unexpectedly in unlikely people—probably lie beyond knowing, and are thus not worth giving a great deal of serious thought to. But the fact that we have been moved to seek, and *do* seek, the grounding in such knowledge of the past, I decided, probably matters a great deal, and not just within the small orbit of living Mays relations. The pursuit of roots, as I've encountered it in the circle of my own kinship—including Aunt Vandalia's—has been surprisingly free of nostalgia, at least of the decadent sort Modernity incites.

Properly understood, however, geneaology can be a way of knowledge, a practice of the examined life. It cannot wholly erase the incurable sense of homelessness we all feel, since that pain is an essential truth of what we are—but this study of the looms on which our language and ideals, even our bones and sinews, were woven may lead to a renewal of *purpose* within the moral wasteland we inhabit. Lewis Lapham, editor of *Harper's*, has remarked that he cannot "help thinking of people without a sense of history as orphans. Deprived of the feeling of kinship with a larger whole and a wider self, and unable to fix their position on the map of time, they don't know that the story in the old books is also their own."

Like the Big House of my childhood's memory, the narratives of any family are endangered by forgetfulness. This is true whether one can track the generations back along stems and branches to roots lying only fifty years deep, or many centuries. Historical inquiry of the sort Lapham proposes can help bring one out of the isolation of forgetting by restoring the sense of that larger Western story to which we belong. But eventually one comes to the end of the road, and of history—to the clearing surrounded by impenetrable forests of forgetfulness, on the edge of which stands the Big House, portal to the deeper memory of the *local*. Here, genealogy can serve, by showing the individual soul the specific story of its formation, how each of us is related to the peculiar movements, patterns of thought, work, and wisdom in which the bodies and minds of us all have been shaped. Genealogy is very much a matter of waiting, and listening for the old stories, lost in the deep bottomlands beyond the end of all roads, to speak.

Of the cultural needs and shocks that turned Edward Mayes, Aunt Vandalia, and myriad other Southerners into genealogists in the 1890s and 1960s, I have already said enough, almost. I would add only one thing: that if their genealogical researches were constricted by fear, they were nevertheless *facing in the right direction*. For they, like the Romans, were correct. In recalling the memories of our dead, we summon up lessons and warnings created in the course of living in a certain place, and examples of how our own moral living can be done.

The best genealogists, I suspect, go out to greet the ancestral spirits as supplicants, seeking such advice for living life honorably and well. They have a connection, however remote, with the Greek poets who first told the tale of Hellen—and, indeed, all who have been weaving legends of origin since the day one tribe of humans encountered another it did not recognize, and asked itself: *Then who are we? What should we now become?*

Sitting on the verandah after Vandalia's burial, and after I had begun thinking on these things, I recalled the ancient request, noted by Mircea Eliade, of the sick in Babylon and Sumer, that the sacred myths of the world's creation and foundation be read to them. Underlying this therapy, Eliade suggests, was the conviction that such recitation would bring the primordial light into the murky, confused present day, *clarifying* the patient, and restoring him to wholeness by exposure to the holiness of the first Dawn. This, or something very close to it, is what Christians believe about the regular, routine enactment of the Divine Mysteries; though Christians certainly hold no copyright on the idea that contact with the Time of Origins can heal, restore, lend clarity.

What clarity came from my first considerations of William Mays? The original dwellings of my family in the New World—the cluster of villages at the mouth of the James, the small tobacco farms roundabout—lay in tiny clearings carved out of the vast Eastern American forests. This obvious fact can be written off as *merely* obvious. Viewed properly, it can open a path through the terrain of Western history, and beyond. For from its very foundations and fulfillment in ancient Greece and Rome, and in the great urban civilizations that flourished and died before the eponymous Hellen sired his three sons, Western civilization has been obsessed by forests. In the long narrative of our relation with Nature, the forests sometimes appear as benign, giving refuge to the wisdom, spontaneity, and beauty we busy civilized folk have all but destroyed in our rush to subdue everything to our whims. This position, important in the Romantic period, and again in the 1960s, is enjoying merely its most recent vogue in the ecological movements of the present day.

Another vision, quite *out* of vogue nowadays—largely in reaction to the older one, but the dominant one in our culture's agenda for many centuries—saw the greenwood as a zone of dark mystery and danger, inhabited by wild semihuman barbarian and savage beasts, requiring extirpation, and even wars of extermination. The latter understanding of the forest was brought to the New World by the earliest colonists in Virginia, along with their Bibles, prayer books, laws, tools, and expectations of plenty and profit. This ideology was to survive for many decades on America's westward-moving frontiers, providing a strangely irrelevant rationale to (for instance) Mississippi settlers for their sweeping devastation of the primeval forests. One would have imagined the practical motive for clearing land in the hills—to earn one's livelihood from crop cultivation—would have been sufficient. But the surviving fireside tales told by pioneers in the Old Southwest are shadowed by the menace of fearsome wolves and huge, man-eating bears, which did not exist outside the imagination of the teller.

In all Faulkner's fiction there is no episode more poignant than the death of Old Ben, the enormous, terrifying bear generations of Yoknapatawpha hunters had been going into the delta canebrakes to track down—who turns out, once dead, to be a small, elderly creature, unimposing, wholly unfearful. But Old Ben's destruction was mandated by the same dreads and radical will to mastery that moved my Virginia ancestors to deforest the newfound land with force altogether in excess of that required by agricultural considerations. An *aesthetic* was at work, inspiring the elimination of all that did not accord with *pure clearing*, of dangerous savages and marauding wild animals alike—everything, in fact, that could cast a shadow on the broad fields in the openings cut into the ancient arboreal darkness.

With the passage of time, however—at least in America's mythological self-understanding—the continental forests were emptied of all dark and danger, the force of rivers and winds and wildlife subdued. And so the United States remained, until recently—when the once-cleared land, the space of the urban and civilized, became again overgrown, dark, dangerous, populated by frightening creatures. Not wolves or bears or aboriginal peoples embodied ultimate menace this time, but the urban poor roaming the city streets at night—their haunt, their version of forest gloom. The electronically alarmed house may not look much like a colonial stockade, but its rationale is the same. Aunt Vandalia's insistence that Uncle Alvin keep a gun handy in case of the break-in she was sure would happen—though no break-in

Tangles, Atlantic coast

had ever happened in Greenwood in living memory—is apparently quite like the fantasy of early Mississipians that, until the wolves were finally eliminated, no baby in its crib was safe. The unpleasant metaphorics of both narratives, if not the details, are the same.

Because it tends to revive at moments when the old, dark forests of unknowing and terror appear to be coming back to retake the cleared land—when, that is, control over the underclass and upstarts is slipping from the hands of those in power—genealogy is often doomed to be a weapon in the war of dying elites against challengers. Even when pursued with most methodical rigor, it usually remains a garden tool for keeping the weeds and wild trees and wild animals—the urgencies of the present moment, that is—away from the house of our reasonable dominion. But it surely can connect us to men and women whose lives provide emblematic witness to the great forces of the West—forces that we, heirs of their blood and spirit, can feel in ourselves, and deal with. The Reverend William Mays, in Virginia *ab origine*, chaplain to the pioneering openers of the dark pagan forests to the bright Eye of God, was possibly a planter and surely the father of planters, on the record as one who stalwartly defended the Virginia Company's right to go on exploiting the land, and emptying it of animals and savages in the name of profit and independence. He was real, and surely left many traces of his passing, now lost to neglect or war. But William is more valuable to the reactionary mind as a paragon of the pious Christian exploiter rather than a historical or even genealogical personage. He fervently pursued his works, both pastoral and profitable, before the most influential Christian thinkers of the early nineteenth century launched their first great crusades against slavery and the subjection of Nature to Man's whim. But English America was created by men of William's sort—Modern people, that is, trying to distance themselves from the past, not find it; establishing a new order in the midst of disarray and dark, and attempting to maintain its purity against contaminations of Old World kings and prelates, and establish a Golden Age of peace and prosperity.

Tell me about the South. What's it like there. What do they do there. What I did there, that warm summer evening on the south verandah of Aunt Vandalia's house, was to begin imagining what it meant to be a scion of this family, a man anchored four hundred years down in time, and in the place, where the men and women of this family put down Modernity's first unperishing roots on this continent. I had before me two books of genesis: Jewell Mayes's tale of four adventurous brothers, and Edward Mayes's gallery of exemplary ancestors. These were the stories to which I belonged, which I could not reject without rejecting myself, and becoming an orphan. But if there were two such books, why could there not be another? One that embraced, for example, the exemplary enterprise in Jewell's Mays folk portraits, and the patrician, Stoic balance celebrated in Edward's more sophisticated verbal drawings—while also engaging the *whole* legacy of my Southern family, dross and gold together?

But by that time—after sorting out, as best I could, the books and dishes, the cluttered, myriad oddments and the confusing genealogical documents heaped everywhere in Aunt Vandalia's crammed Greenwood house—the last thing on my mind was reading more about Mays folk and Mays places.

Readers since the studious desert fathers of the early Church have known the sin of a dry spirit, into which pondering books can pitch us when reading ceases to be an enlargement of the mental world, and turns into an arid substitute for it. Seeing exactly this precipice up ahead, I dumped my aunt's genealogical papers into boxes and took them, along with the other mementos and memorabilia we were hauling away, back north and home, where they were promptly shelved far back in a high cupboard. The realm of knowledge this evidence had opened to me—the South as idea and place, the zone my ancestors cleared of forest darkness, dwelt and brought forth children in, and stamped with memorials of their passing—had simply grown tiresome to think about.

But the files did not slip quickly from my waking mind, as I had thought they might, once I'd returned to my usual work of writing art criticism. Those transcribed wills and deeds, family trees and such rested unquietly in their obscure nook in the overhauled factory I live in, whispering questions much like those Shreve McCannon had put to Quentin Compson in their Harvard rooms. *Where did it all begin? What's it like there? What is it to be there?*

Faced with such insistent queries, I could make only one decision, and so made it: to travel to American destinations certainly never before on my wish-list itinerary, and on it now only because I imagined that answers of some sort waited for me in those towns and rural regions of the South. I did not yet know exactly where I would wind up these journeyings, but the first place to go was not hard to settle on. After all, for anyone inclined to answer the questions that emerged from my weariness with paper genealogy, for anyone who wants to track the inward trace of English-speaking America's first ancestors, history begins at Hampton.

3

THE PEACEABLE KINGDOM

Nursery, Shreveport

THE CHESAPEAKE BAY CITY OF HAMPTON, WHICH STANDS WHERE William Mays's tiny congregation of farmers, tradesfolk, and militia met for prayer in the early seventeenth century, is today a vague, dilapidated smudge on the tip of a long peninsula, extending from the mainland toward the sea between the York and James rivers. It's a blighted town of the mindlessly planned, or aggressively unplanned, sort typical of the industrialized New South, puddling toward the horizon until exhausted or abandoned—though, in this case, the vegetative creep to which North American cities are prone has been arrested by two mighty facts. One is water, which surrounds the near-island town site on three sides. The other is the complex of forbidden military emplacements, including Langley Air Force Base and the U.S. Naval Weapons Station, that occupy great expanses of the peninsula's land mass. To approach Hampton from Richmond and the northwest on the interstate highway at night, as I did, is to run a hideous, brilliantly spotlighted gauntlet of huge advertisements for the food and shelter franchises at upcoming interchanges. To turn off the expressway into Hampton's center—surrounded by the dark expanses of water and war preparation—is to find oneself in the familiar, ominous quiet of abandoned downtowns throughout contemporary America.

Which is, I jotted down in my notebook the first night of my stay in Hampton, exactly as the place should be. While Puritan William was probably exiled to the dismal company settlement in Virginia, he might at least take consolation in his distance from the crass king's British Babylon, with its fabulous masques, public pomps, and spiritual corruption. But the damp, forested point of land held out little consolation, and much practical challenge, for the Englishmen recruited by the Virginia Company for resettlement on America's Atlantic tidewater. They had come out for economic opportunity. And if profit meant—as it did, to their minds—hacking down the ancient forests for firewood and building materials, and destroying any troublesome humans or animals who were luckless enough to be where the newcomers wanted to build and live, then so be it. To such men, the cry of Nietzsche's Zarathustra—"Remain faithful to the earth!"—or the similar appeals of contemporary ecologists, would have seemed contradictory; for the earth, the *natural*, was the old enemy they had come to subdue.

It could hardly have been otherwise. The first Virginians were not learned, by and large, and most of the men had been charmed by the Virginia Company from apprenticeships in England's crowded port cities. Their nearness to the natural, wild world, vanquished in England centuries before their time, can only have revived and intensified in them the ancient European suspicion and fear of forests, and the readiness to chop them down. Anyway, the oceangoing British fleet required timbers, and getting them made the destruction of forests necessary, and something akin to a patriotic duty. None would have heard of, let alone would have read, the serious proposals for methodical land management making the rounds of the elite in late Elizabethan times. And the enterprising souls who came after the royal revocation of the Virginia Company's charter in 1624 built on these violent foundations, squeezing fortunes from the land within a transplanted culture that encouraged such liberation of the earth from forest dark. The congregation in the care of William Mays after 1609, located near a little wilderness settlement of the Kecoughtan aboriginals, was no more stymied by reservations about their rough *modus operandi* than their latter-day republican successors in the city appear to be.

In the midst of Hampton's inner wasteland of parking lots, the dignified presence of St. John's Episcopal Church strikes a beautifully discordant chord. The brick edifice is late, dating only from 1728. Throughout the era of company management, William's worshippers had no meeting place, but gathered for the offices of the Established Church in a house. In 1623, just before the end of company rule, a little frame structure with a brick floor was built, and stood until its demolition in 1698, when another wooden house of prayer was erected. But while William Mays never ministered there, the stately brick edifice houses the memorials and memories of his service, kept alive over four centuries by generations of my Anglican kindred— the great family in which I will always belong more essentially, in my mind, than to any people named Mays.

That *belonging* abruptly came home to me on a spring Sunday morning, while I was offering prayers and thanksgivings with other believers who had gathered for the Holy Eucharist at St. John's. I had come to this lovely church, with its rational, earthbound cruciform exterior and interior of delicate, decorated American Victorian woodwork, to find whatever traces might remain of my ultimate North American ancestor in the bricks, monuments, and records preserved in that place. As far as all that was concerned, I was not disappointed. St. John's is an attic of recollections about the congregation's origins, tribulations, overcomings. There is a splendid window, installed in 1903 by the Association for the Preservation of Virginia Antiquities, listing the colonial clergy, headed by my ancestor. There is a memorial dedicated to Virginia Laydon, believed to be the first child born of English parents in the New World, and surely, with her parents, a member of the parish. And there are memorials here of the three deliberate guttings of the church's interior: during the Revolutionary conflict, again in the War of 1812, and finally in the first year of the Civil War, this time by Hampton's own Rebel population, determined to leave not even their most ancient church intact, lest the invading army of the Union find some use for it.

During the service in Hampton, however, I began to wonder whether anything I might learn at St. John's about the lives and mentalities formed within my Southern family over centuries, or about even the South itself, could ever be as compelling as the Eucharist, or the living contemporary fellowship in whose midst I celebrated it. But I had long before found—with no slight intended to documentary genealogists who seek out such buildings, or the architectural aficionados who cherish them—that places of prayer, however venerable and magnificent, never involved me as deeply as the people who keep alive the living truth of Christianity within them.

That conviction was set on fire in me the first time I set foot in an Episcopal church, when I was seventeen. It was a small and impressive edifice in an Arkansas university town. The service was a plain, routine reading of Morning Prayer; the anthems (as I recall) were ill-sung, the organ wheezy and out of tune. I have forgotten what the sermon was about. What I do remember is that this first encounter with Anglicanism was a step into a world larger and more profound than any I had ever known, and infinitely more full of joy than anything I had experienced in my distraught life up to this time. On that Sunday, I resolved to join that wider world. In the week following, I began to study the Anglican way, its history and doctrine, and its continuities—uncrippled even by the tumults of Reformation—with the primordial Catholic spirituality and teaching brought from Rome to my Anglo-Saxon ancestors some fourteen centuries before by St. Augustine of Canterbury. While I had always thought of myself as a Christian, in the general way one does when raised in pervasively Christian Southern culture, I had never before been deeply struck by the astonishing beauty and intelligence of Christendom, its deep harmony that, on a Sunday in Arkansas, seemed *right.* To this day— despite many seasons of doubt and mental illness that, many times, has swept away almost everything else I believed and hoped in, despite much change in my paths of Christian thinking—I have never forgotten the grandeur, inner music, and glory of the church I first glimpsed nearly forty years ago.

The Eucharist at St. John's Church reminded me of these things, which, in turn, made me begin to wonder about my reasons for coming there. I had come seeking the dead, but had found the living. I had come to meet an elusive Anglican clergyman and kinsman of the seventeenth century, and had discovered, instead, a vivid assembly of Christians with whom I was connected far more fully. During the final prayers and blessings, the thought came to me that the project of finding ancestral roots, begun in Aunt Vandalia's house not long before, might be misguided after all.

I was prepared to drive off, and out of Hampton, back north toward Toronto. But, as it happened, I stopped after the service to speak with the rector, Mr. Rodney L. Caulkins, and explain my visit. Mr. Caulkins, I found, was accustomed to having Mays antiquarians pitch up at St. John's, looking for the earliest occupant of his job in the parish. He was helpful, supplying me with historical handouts about the present building and its three predecessors, and telling me of the near-collapse of the congregation during the fifty years following the Revolution, when local republicans were hostile to everything smacking of Englishry, especially imperial Anglicanism's clergy and houses of worship.

What most firmly snagged my attention during our chat, however, was not Mr. Caulkins's polite, routine talk to yet another seeker for old William. It was his description of the state of the parish in 1980, when he was called there to be rector. St. John's was ailing. The old Episcopalian families in the neighborhood, many of whom could trace their affiliation with the parish far back into the eighteenth century, were dying off or moving away from decrepit Hampton; and few young people were coming along to take their places. The congregation was facing a stark alternative: to struggle on against financial shortfalls and declining membership, keeping itself going, somehow, as a worshipping Episcopalian community—though just how this was to be done, nobody knew—or to give up and hand over the building to an antiquarian or historical society, which would then operate it as yet another museum of colonial America. When the day was done, however, the congregation decided, by the grace of God, to go on. And to help them do so, they called upon Mr. Caulkins, the energetic priest in charge of a prosperous suburban congregation near Washington.

At first, he balked at the invitation. St. John's was famous in the Episcopal Church, both for its antiquity—the congregation is the oldest in New World Anglicanism south of Newfoundland—and in the Diocese of Virginia for its remorselessly declining health. Understandably, Mr. Caulkins did not want to be the priest who presided at the funeral of so venerable a parish church, and certainly not the man who let the fine brick building become a tourist attraction and focus for Colonial Era nostalgia. But in the end, he decided to come, and pitch his energies into making St. John's come alive again; which it did, and has continued to do ever since. When I visited Hampton, fifteen years after Mr. Caulkins's installation as rector, the people of St. John's were obviously thriving in this old home of Christian worship, with old-timers and newcomers mixing promisingly, and the church anything but a museum.

The world map I carry around in my head has always been dotted with such Anglican churches, and churches of other and all sorts. When on the road during the vacation season or for my newspaper, I rarely miss church—not out of any sense of grim obligation to baptismal promises, but merely because of the unfailing pleasure of worship with Christians of my own or some other rite of Christendom. In that hour of Sunday worship, St. John's had become yet another sacred place I have worshipped in and would cherish, but it had also become something more than that—a bright point on the newer map I was starting to draw of Mays kin and sites that lay behind me in time, and among which I belong.

What made St. John's an especially important star on this new chart I was drafting was the fact that it was *alive*—not another genealogical repository of crackled documents and rusty artifacts lying in vitrines, but a living legacy from William Mays, who, in the perpetual giving and gift of the assembly who had met in this place at least since 1609, had himself continued to live on there, and within the contemporary world. Nothing could be more remote in spirit from the singing, praying congregation of St. John's—certainly as crabby and holy, distracted and tragic and joyful, contradictory and contrary and embedded in time and circumstances and nonsense as any other Christian assembly, and altogether lovable in that humanity—than the rarefied "colonial shrine" that the more pessimistic parishioners had proposed years before. Had the parish come to that end, I would have certainly found evidence of the Reverend William Mays there—though not a real person to whom I am joined in blood and time, but a distant mummy plastered inside the Hollywood-antique costumery and pretty Technicolor scenery of Colonial Era myth.

That myth had been a problem for me long before the start of my genealogical ramblings. The first time I studied the history of pre-Revolutionary America, while still in high school, the pious tale and imagery of bewigged colonials struck me as banal and absurd, hence quenching any curiosity about this American era I might have felt. I should add that the animus I felt had to do with my conversion to Communism shortly before. It came upon me in my fifteenth summer, when, on a visit to the house in Greenwood and suffering the extreme inner agitation that (I now know) often comes with chronic depression, I decided not to return to the relation who had most recently been looking after me, and to finish my education at Greenwood School. While settling in among the grandmother, aunt, and uncle, I escaped into two books. Dale Carnegie's *How To Win Friends and Influence People*, I imagined, would give me the key to happiness that had eluded me throughout my life after leaving Spring Ridge. (It did not do so.) The other book was an edition of *Capital*, and *The*

Communist Manifesto. Enchanted more by the ferocious poetry of Marx's language than by his propositions, I determined then and there to give my life to Marxist-Leninist struggle.

But among my motives for becoming a revolutionary—if I can sort them out now from the intense turmoil and confusion of that summer—was surely intellectual delight in Marx's brilliant diagnosis of industrial Modernity's spiritual and social illness. This delight has not gone away; I am as convinced as ever about the great power of Marx's explanation of the Modern condition. But the more immediate cause for my attraction to Marxist certainty and purpose emerged from isolation, raw *interiority*—the painful longing for reunion with some larger world that I had not experienced since leaving my father's plantation, and would eventually find, first in Anglicanism, and later in contemporary philosophy, theology, art, and literature. All that, however, still lay firmly in the future. When I was fifteen, no desire or inclination, no state of mind I experienced seemed to connect to the ordinary world. So, in the way of neurotics, I responded to this sense of alienation by constructing for myself an identity as the most alienated creature imaginable: a Red in a small-town Southern school during the Cold War, when vicious postwar Red-baiting was enjoying the end of its long heyday in the United States.

What little I knew, or thought I knew, about Marx-Engels-Lenin Thought can be summed up in the proposition that the will to revolution springs from the "objective" discontent of the industrial proletariat, whose productive strength had been created by the very plutocrats now trying to keep it docile by means of bribes and terror. Which, from my high school standpoint, more or less described America in 1776: an imperial outpost divided between a population of prosperous native farmers, merchants, and industrialists, and a small cadre of armed imperialists bent on maintaining the enshacklement of their wealthy American colonies to the world commodities market headquartered in London. But I had also understood from Marx—or, more accurately, from reading about the Bolshevik Revolution—that the best way to prevent the return of elite marauding was to extirpate the ruling class forcibly, and vilify them afterward. It was something republican Americans, absurdly, seemed not to have done. (I did not yet know about the persecution and revolutionary terror unleashed after 1780 against Loyalists—a few highly placed, the vast majority farmers and small-town folk much like my own ancestors, thousands and thousands of whom were forced to flee into Canada and exile farther abroad.)

I could grasp the point of America's ritual devotion to black-hatted seekers of religious freedom in seventeenth-century Massachusetts, and pre-Revolutionary pioneers clad in animal skins and driving their ox teams into the continental interior. Such fiercely independent people were, or were said to be, the spiritual precursors of Minutemen. What I, a Communist, could not comprehend was the lingering, egregious attachment of Americans to the life-styles of the corrupt and cruel colonial elite we had overthrown. Evidence of such piety was everywhere. Before the Second World War, and with a vengeance after it, flimsy replicas of Colonial mansions, with skinny pillars holding aloft streamlined pediments, were going up across the South. Colonial "elegance" and "tradition," as embodied in curved-leg chairs and hutches and coffee tables, lamps, and even "formal" landscaping were *la moda* in the South, at least among the newly rich, and survivors of the Depression enriched by the wartime economy. On the suburbanizing outskirts of towns across America were Colonial Heights, Colonial Hills, even Colonial Malls. (Why, I recall thinking, no *Revolutionary* Heights?) And for the newly mobilized, vacationing multitudes after the Second World War, there were the "Colonial" pilgrimages, which allowed lowly folk to step inside the very draped and chandeliered rooms where our Betters had lived out their Elegant and Traditional Colonial Lives.

To this day, the most popular destination for white Americans hankering for the fantasy of colonial rural graciousness lies only a few miles upriver from the parking lots and malls of Hampton and adjacent Newport News. "Colonial Williamsburg," as this curious modern pastiche advertises itself, stands where Virginia's governors reigned from 1699 until 1775, when the last of them fled for his life. This tourism enterprise delights visitors with recorder recitals, candlelight tours, and performances of the Virginia Garrison Regiment and Field Musick, oyster pie, people bustling around in "authentic" costumery. But for those who make the pilgrimage, and find themselves impatient with the grating quaintness of Colonial Williamsburg, the plantations on the north side of the James, between highway and river, offer surely the most cherished recollection of a gracious, patrician America, now vanished under malls and into the bright culture of speed.

The country is low there, without the hills rising beyond the fall line—a land crossed by narrow creeks emptying into the James, and dented by swamps and creek bottoms dense and forbidding. Turning south off Highway 5 anywhere, one crosses the broad fields of old farms before coming to the James, wide and slow and dark, channeling Virginia's fresh inland waters to the sea—the James, a river but once also a road, a broad band of light between widely distant banks, the great link in pacified Virginia between the colonial planters and the imperial administration situated at marshy, riverside Jamestown until 1698, when it moved to Williamsburg.

Of all the plantations on the James, and probably anywhere in the South, Westover is the most famous, and the one most enduringly tinctured by the aristocratic and antirepublican hues much favored by republican Americans. The site was chosen in 1619 to be the seat of Henry West, heir of the third Lord De La Warr, though it quickly passed from noble hands into common ones. The first William Byrd, enriched through trade, bought the land in 1688, but it was his son William (1674–1744), the distinguished diarist, traveler, and book collector, who brought into existence the present miniaturized English manor house. Westover today (unlike its architectural near-contemporary, St. John's Church at Hampton) is unfortunately without reason to exist apart from its importance to tourists and architectural connoisseurs. Its proportions may once have been lovely, though somewhat jarring to modern eyes, for the two wings now bridged to the central block were originally disjunct. What we have at Westover today is less a relic of Colonial architecture and landscape planning than a memorial to the way preservationists and connoisseurs of Quaint around the turn of the century thought a plantation grandee's house *should* look.

My Virginia ancestors in the early eighteenth century and beyond saw it as it was in the beginning. Plying the busy water road of the James between Williamsburg and their plantations and commercial interests a few miles upriver on the Appomattox, John Maies's sons would have often passed the stately face of the house, oriented firmly toward the river. The rear, from which visitors in our own day customarily approach, is architecturally indifferent, with all the charm and light drama reserved for the river view, which is as it should have been. For, to the mind of the younger William Byrd, and in the minds of the colony's planters, Westover was less house than monument, a tribute to wealth, ambition, and high English civilization that was *intended* to be appreciated by its owner's fellow colonials, and emulated.

The Westover *ésprit* did not, of course, feature the nostalgic agrarianism the mansion powerfully later evoked for industrialized, urban Americans; for, in Byrd's era, almost everyone in the colony farmed, or did business with the planters scattered alongside its rivers. Westover did, however, advertise to the Virginia planters an ideal of a *way to be* a planter—one that Byrd and others in his elite company of prosperous farmers impressed deeply, and forever, on the mind of the South. Its contents are today recalled nowhere better than on the gravestone of the house's famous master, in Byrd's formal garden, restored around 1900. Composed probably in our own century, with a bit too much *Masterpiece Theatre* period style, the epitaph is not about the Byrd who actually lived—every inch an Englishman of the colony, who *did*, and prospered grandly from his land speculation, tobacco farming, and other enterprises—but about a man who, supremely, *was*. His father, we read, sent him to England to study, where he achieved "a happy Proficiency in polite and various learning." He was called to the bar and spent time in the Low Countries, later becoming member and finally president of the Council of the Colony. "To all this were added a great Elegancy of Taste and Life, the well-bred Gentleman and polite Companion, the splendid Oeconomy and prudent Father of a Family."

Here, American imagination has vaporized William Byrd into a wisp of allegory, glowing softly in a pseudo-old garden he would never have recognized. I had known burning reality in Hampton, the reality of compelling *kinship*, in both blood and religion. Expunged from this verbal picture on the tombstone was the more complex iconography of Westover—the silent cry of human slavery upon which the Byrds' wealth, and my family's, was founded, the destruction of the aboriginals, still unfinished in the seventeenth and early eighteenth centuries. The epitaph represents the *rewriting* of early Virginia experience to fit contemporary yearning, and, for that reason, is false.

But, as I realized when leaving Westover's grounds, not *wholly* false. By the soft spring morning I turned off Highway 5 to visit the house, the simplistic Marxism of my fifteenth year was decades behind me, and so also, I hope, was the intolerant (and largely intolerable) teenager I had been. Too, living in decaying late-industrial American cities had left me better equipped to understand why Americans want, perhaps even *need*, the temporary escape offered by the James River tour. But despite that distance of years, my condescension toward modern taste for the "Colonial" (and the architecture, furniture, and theme parks, such as Williamsburg, invented to gratify it) had abated very little, perhaps because I had really never had occasion to question it. Then, as I was turning up the drive back toward the highway, close on a hundred elegantly tailored pilgrims were emptied from their tour bus to pay homage to the highest of colonial Virginia's planter autocrats. Was there any contradiction in their minds, I wondered, about just what they were doing there? About the respects they were paying to everything the more radical proponents of Revolution wished to undo, the durable accomplishments of Tory architecture and colonial Tory ideals of decorum and intellectual cultivation, the imitation of Roman worthies hallowed in Tory memory?

Almost certainly not. But did that matter? I, too, was on a pilgrimage of sorts, in search of the land of ancestors who had lived through the South's first century and a half, and of clues to the consciousness and strategies of living devised among them on the Virginia earth. Mere demythologizing of the colonial myth might be entertaining—for somebody else to do, I suppose. But allowing myself to slide back easily into smug contempt, long buried (because I had been long out of the South), or letting myself drift into the remythologizing that tempts all Southern explorers of family history—the subtle elevation of the ancestors from ordinary people into paragons—would have suffocated any hope of achieving what I really wanted: an understanding of my place, and that of my family, in the geography of American imagination. But, as I discovered, it's "Colonial Williamsburg" that is thoroughly fake, not Westover. The best values embodied in Westover's symmetry and serene nobility were engraved deeply on Southern culture even before there was a separate American region called "the South"—when Virginia was still the very heart of England's North American civilization. They were incorporated by my ancestors on the rivers into their lives, as the right way to be; and passed down through the generations, in stories and by example. Along the line of that continuity of ideals, it's a very short distance from the mental world of William Byrd and John Maies to that of my grandfather John and his wife, Sister Erin, and even that of my father and Aunt Vandalia. The opening of wider distance, I gradually decided on the road west toward Richmond from the James River plantations, had begun with me—though this gap I felt between my soul and the souls of my ancestors was still not too wide to be bridged; and it was to do so that I was there, thinking of the South, driving slowly through the fields and bottoms of the land on which my family's mind assumed enduring form.

The land John Maies patented in 1668 lies atop a high headland over the Appomattox River, which bends sharply, broadens, and slows there in its approach to the James, about three miles downstream. The site lies between Hopewell and Petersburg, both slumping into the decay typical of New South cities grown elderly, and into the urban topography of *nowhere, anywhere*. Neither town would still exist, perhaps, were it not for the two principal businesses of the area, both situated on the high fields of John Maies and his planter neighbors in the seventeenth century. The Fort Lee Military Reservation occupies territory that would be ominous even without the menacing signage—an eerily flat, vacant place, clear-cut except for a few forlorn stands of trees along the roadside, dotted by buildings of indecipherable function. North of the military land, closer to the river's rounded bend and on the very ground John Maies plowed, sprawls the campus of the United States Bureau of Prisons' Federal Correctional Institution, fenced round with coils of concertina wire spiked with razorlike metal shards. Between them, Mars and Saturn—red god of war, and the leaden lord of restriction—had desolated the river overlook long before I got there, shaved off its topsoil, erased every mark of any presence except their own.

But I did not come to this spot expecting a stately home, or a pioneer cabin, or any other artifact left behind by my ancestors. If I brought any mental image at all to this place, it was a lonely, emptied field running out to a jagged lip of weed, then dropping off

steeply to the silted-up Appomattox. But Americans rarely just aban-
don a place, allowing it to slide into dereliction and find its own
place in reality's shift, turn, and quietude. And if the slide is indeed
allowed to go on for even a little while, there remains in the end a
single alternative: erasure of every trace of what went before and the
raising of something new; or architectural taxidermy of the sort that
keeps Westover standing for the tourists. Long ago, the decision was
made to erase what stood on the headland.

Still, I wanted to know what it looked like, and what relationship
John Maies's farmland bore to its vicinity. Prevented from standing
on his ground by military fences, kept away by prison guards and
postings—a sign at the gatehouse of the penitentiary declares, oddly:
No Spandex!—I crossed to the *north* side of the Appomattox and
looked for a viewing spot close to the river, only to get lost again and
again. I might eventually have stopped looking, had I not by chance
found a back street on the river's steep north bank, lined with little
bungalows under construction. Across the sluggish Appomattox,
clogged with silt islands, lay a sight of the prison grounds more
impressive than I had expected. The land of old William Maies, his
son John, and their successors commanded the great flat prominence, descending steeply to the river on three sides.

As I took in the view, it occurred to me that there was something
more significant about John Maies's land than its spacious prospect.
The place on which my ancestor lived, worked, and, about 1713,
died a very old man stands between two worlds, defined then and
now by a geological configuration hardly less crucial than the Rock-
ies to the settlement of the American land. Virginians call it the fall
line. Running roughly north-south across the state, top to bottom, it
is the long boundary at which the hills of the piedmont meet the flat
tidewater, and the eastward flows of Virginia's parallel rivers,
grooved deep by the waters they carry from the Appalachians, empty
into the slower, wider estuaries, including the James, that spend
themselves at last into Chesapeake Bay. While John lived, a gulf
inexpressible in mileage, and crucial to the future of American civilization, lay along Virginia's fall line.

Downriver and east of it, and of John's plantation, was Bermuda
City (now City Point), a settlement laid out in 1613 on the James
River by Sir Thomas Gates, and the community in which John may

have grown to manhood. Only a few miles farther down from Bermuda City, on the low country's flat bottoms of clay, sand, and marl, stood the plantation from which John Rolfe harvested the first commercial crop of *Nicotiana tabacum*. By the time a seventeenth-century navigator, floating downstream, reached Varina Farm, he would be in the heartland of the prosperous, conventional Virginian civilization to which John belonged as heir and native son, into which the first sparks of the European Enlightenment were falling. The remarkable thing is that Virginia was ready for this fire fall. In considerably less than a century after their arrival, the English settlers' ignorant attempts to bring forth exotic fruit from the plain Virginia soil were over, the principles of sound crop cultivation established and well understood, and the fears of starvation, which had haunted my earliest ancestors in America, eliminated. The English Civil War, the short-lived British republic, and the Restoration had come and gone, with little effect on the colony's steadily rising fortunes, and deepening social stability.

Learning was not new in the Virginia colony toward the end of the seventeenth century, when John was nearing the end of his active career as a planter and land speculator; George Sandys had translated Ovid's *Metamorphoses* into heroic couplets there as early as 1626. But the *new* learning—springing from all educated Europe's renewed fascination with the literature, institutions, and aristocratic republicanism of ancient Rome—was to inscribe itself indelibly on the Southern mind, simply by quickly becoming the first conscious, concrete idealism in Virginia high culture.

Among the seven books given by Governor Francis Nicholson to the recently founded College of William and Mary in 1695—a year when the Puritans were drowning women for witches in Salem, it's perhaps worth noting—was John Locke's *Some Thoughts Concerning Education*, published in London two years earlier. But even before the governor offered this critical fruit to the sons of the colony's planters, the ideals of Locke and the practice of new science were circulating among the mercantile and agricultural gentry of the colonial capital and beyond, and meeting approval. Toward the end of Britain's first imperial century on the rivers emptying into Chesapeake Bay, literate farmers had Sir Francis Bacon's essays and Sir Thomas More's *Utopia* in their libraries. Mrs. Sarah Willoughby (a kinswoman of Joe Chandler) had stocked her plantation house with serious modern texts on topics ranging from midwifery and exotic travel to navigation, geography, and the correct cultivation of mulberry trees.

The ideas in Locke's revolutionary *Two Treatises on Government*, published in 1690, were well planted on the James by 1700 in the magnificent library of William Byrd, and in the broadly influential political thinking of its master. Sedition, let alone open revolution, was not yet on anybody's mind in royal Virginia. But in the house of Byrd and among educated men like him, the literary formulations of a new social existence were taking shape, patrician and agrarian in outline—a magnificent, backward-yearning attempt by intelligent men to re-create on the James the great original stamped on their dreams: the astonishing republic of farmers and aristocrats that had arisen on the Tiber, and re-created the world.

Sailing up the James from the open fields of the Enlightenment tidewater, and only a few miles west on the Appomattox beyond John Maies's hilltop farm, the navigator would reach, quite literally, the end of the world. Beyond the fall line lay the stony upcountry of central Virginia, gashed by rivers descending through gulches of Precambrian granite mantled by loam. At the turn of the eighteenth century, the terrain was a still a wild, largely unknown wilderness, haunted by the great animals that had dwelt on it since the last Ice Age, and shadowed by forest darkness, beyond which lay the remote mountains of the continental interior. In the time of John's sons, these lands would be opened for land speculation by low-country entrepreneurs such as the Byrds, and for clearing and farming by newcomers—first, still English; and later, Scots-Irish. The fall line, that is, would cease to mark a fixed limit, and become a frontier, moving with the tide of land-hungry immigrants—people who had crossed an ocean, and were now pressing west across the seventeenth-century boundary of European civilization into the piedmont.

But for John Maies—as for many other native-born Virginians of English background, and with family land and old, local loyalties— destiny lay in staying put, sinking roots even deeper into the soil. The fluorescence of learning that came to Virginia in the wake of wealth shone most brightly at Williamsburg, and among its high circles of officialdom; but it was hardly confined to the colonial headquarters. John Maies and his sons William and Daniel may not have owned copies of the social and historical treatises coming with hogs and other supplies on English ships putting in at ports along the James. What matters is that they lived within a mental world infused by thought at once innovative and deeply conservative. And within the social contract now settled in Virginia—at least in the light of the documentary fragments that have survived America's periodic civil convulsions—my ancestors' tenure on the fall-line plantations had come to mirror, with an almost uncanny accuracy, the reign of peaceable virtues predicted by ancient writers and their Enlightenment followers. If the stability of Mays ancestors and kin—their staying put on the same land over generations and willingness to stay in one place—can be admitted into evidence, we can only conclude that they experienced the present less as a tight, difficult point between past and future—our experience of duration both at the end of the twentieth century, and at the time those first unsure English settlers came ashore on this continent—than as a small, sunny field bounded by civil peace and secured by law.

But in that open pasture of time early in the century of Enlightenment, the Maies planters were kept busy by the one thing that mattered most to them, and on which all their hope and prosperity rested: land. This much we know from the numerous, sporadic flashes of my ancestors' names on the pages of the legal record, appearing like sparks hit off a smoldering log by a quick movement of power and money—a transfer of property, deed, or will specifying the disposition of farmland, record of payment made, a patent, a land-deal partnership struck or dissolved. The name of John Maies flickers for an instant in the documentary record of Charles City County, some ten miles inland from James Towne along the James, on October 18, 1658: "Jno. Maies. Paid 100 lbs of tobacco for 1 wolfe." On March 11, 1663, one Thomas Benington transferred power of attorney to "my loving friend John Mayes to collect debts and sell goods sent in ships to Virginia." In a land transfer dated April 20, 1680, he appears fleetingly as a neighbor—in another as an owner, in yet another a seller; but continually involved in the orderly flow of lands and goods on which the colony's prosperity rested.

The ancestors and relations who left these traces were neither grand planters of the tidewater nor inland pioneers, but settled, successful farming folk who stayed in the vicinity of the emerging towns, overland routes, and river roads such as the Appomattox, on which their tobacco was hauled downstream to port on fresh water and out to the world markets on salt. In this satisfaction with their circumstances on the Virginia headland at the fall line, my Maies ancestors were *ordinary* people of their time—not particularly memorable to their descendants, well-knit with their neighbors on the river, not grand, and apparently not wishing to be.

And, eventually, at least some were illiterate. That much we learn from a document signed on a November day in 1711, when John's son Daniel marked his name with an *X*. Rightly understood, this tiny fact cannot be taken as evidence that Daniel Maies was ignorant in any matter *other* than his letters, or that his family had begun a slide into some kind of degraded rural primitivism. We know from the ample documentary production of the era that lawyers and the clerks of Church of England parishes served enterprising planters such as the Maies family as scribes, writing down what needed to be written down, mostly vital records and transactions. Daniel's *X* suggests that, without knowing it and surely without designing to do so, the secure Virginia planters of the third and fourth generations after 1609 were evolving a new civilization in America, both politically stable and economically free—and illiterate.

Only modern prejudice makes such a civilization seem abhorrent. But a culture not very different from that constructed by ordinary Virginia farmers—the Greek world in the glorious fifth century B.C.— stands at the very fountainhead of the Western intelligence. As he emerges from the pages of the classicist Eric A. Havelock's landmark *Preface to Plato,* the ordinary Athenian citizen in the time of Plato and Aristotle had little use for literacy. Not because he chose ignorance, but merely because he carried around in his head the sustaining myths, laws, and other cultural mechanisms of social being. For the Greeks in this remarkable moment, the whole technology of complex recollection—crucial to every known human society—was *acoustic,* not *literate.* Everything we consider necessary for responsible civic life—morality and history, a sense of one's place in family and nation, laws, even the techniques of shipbuilding and other industrial crafts—was handed down orally from one generation to the next by specialized orators, who were themselves illiterate, though proficient in effective performance. Education involved the commitment of these matters to memory, by rote repetition of, principally, the Homeric epics and Hesiod, and the frequent refreshment of memory by hearing these poems sung again and again, at banquets and special presentations—all of it, to keep alive the shared codes of identity. "The colloquial word-of-mouth which in our own culture is able to serve the uses of even important human transactions," writes Havelock, "remains effective only because there exists in the background, often unacknowledged, some written frame of reference or court of appeal, a memorandum or document or book. The memoranda of a culture of wholly oral communication are inscribed in the rhythms and formulas imprinted on the living memory."

The whole business was repugnant to Plato, who argued that true, free thought was impossible when the mind was stuffed with traditional formulas and aphorisms and narratives—and who taught our teachers, down through the history of Western civilization, to believe the same thing. But this is not the place to rehearse the cultural dynamic of ancient Athenian civilization as Havelock explains it, or Plato's durable critique of it. It is enough to note that the illiterate culture evolving along Virginia's rivers at the turn of the eighteenth century seems to have been similarly acoustic, with the stories of Holy Scripture, read publicly week by week during mandatory services, in place of Homer, and sermons in the place of Hesiod. The peaceable character of Virginian civilization at this moment raises an almost heretical question. Can it be that Plato was wrong? That, in fact, liberty and literacy are indeed contradictory?

In a brilliant aside spun out in his memoir *Tristes Tropiques,* the anthropologist Claude Lévi-Strauss reminds us that the tremendous advances in agriculture achieved by the first farmers of the ancient Near East had been accumulated and passed down over eons in the absence of writing. Of course, without such systematic knowledge of land and plants, hybridization and knowledge of the ways of livestock, settled farm life would never have come into existence; and we European humans might still be nomads following the great herds for food, as we had been for hundreds of thousands of years before the Neolithic revolution in farming technology. On the basis of the dramatic change in human life wrought by that revolution, and the long, peaceful interval of settlement that accompanied and followed it, Lévi-Strauss concludes that, rather than preceding our passage to stable, coherent material culture, writing comes *after* it—at the very point, in fact, that the relatively peaceful farming world is giving way to war-making civilizations.

Lévi-Strauss notes that, during writing's debut in the ancient world from the Nile to China, "the one phenomenon which has invariably accompanied it is the formation of cities and empires"— systems of dictatorial, integrated control, the establishment of a rigidly hierarchical class structure. His conclusion, made in the light of the bald facts in subsequent history, is that the emergence of writing everywhere has seemed "to favour rather the exploitation than the enlightenment of mankind." Reading becomes mandatory, that is, when the ruling powers decide that everyone must know the rules and codes, and that all unofficial languages and forms of thought outside the official ones must be drained of power, thus depriving the citizenry of mental hiding places from the intrusion of total administration. On balance, he further decides, "the primary function of writing, as a means of communication, is to facilitate the enslavement of other human beings."

Such startling, Orwellian convictions lead effortlessly to the last chapter of Lévi-Strauss's book, and its famous and profound homage to Rousseau. If ancient myth told the eighteenth-century *philosophe* that we humans once enjoyed a golden, fruitful age from which we've declined to our sorry, overcivilized present state, twentieth-century prehistorical study not only confirms it, but also identifies the place and time. The brief historical period of accomplished farming, before writing emerged, was the one that embodied best Rousseau's understanding of humankind's happiest and most desirable state. When the philosopher celebrated this "middle ground," writes Lévi-Strauss, "I am inclined to think that he was right. In the Neolithic age, Man had already made most of the inventions which are indispensable to his security . . . had put himself beyond the reach of cold and hunger; he acquired leisure to think"—precisely the liberty to think at ease, uninhibited by hectic urban existence, that is central to every pastoral ideal of good and happy life.

Not long after my stay in the southside Virginia vicinity of John Maies's land and river, I was dispatched by my newspaper to

Philadelphia, and the city's Museum of Art, to review a retrospective of Paul Cézanne that was concluding its transatlantic tour there. I had no idea, while flying down for the show early that morning, that the day in Philadelphia would include not merely the most breathtaking encounter with Cézanne's painting I had ever known, but also a revelation about another artist, an American this time, whom I thought had simply nothing to reveal.

His name is Edward Hicks. Perhaps the most famous version of his oft-repeated composition called *The Peaceable Kingdom* hangs in the Museum of Art among the antique clocks and side tables and Gilded Age bric-a-brac of the sort that ornament the novels of Edith Wharton. I did not go looking for the Hicks work at the end of my day with Cézanne. The painting just appeared, I recall, as I was wandering in the general direction of the rooms where the canvases and logic-bending sculptures of Marcel Duchamp are kept.

I was surprised by the Hicks, if only because, until that day, I'd thought the nineteenth-century amateur and his gently apocalyptic picture of the lion lying down with the lamb had been long ago banished to the misty, distant isle of "folk art," where art critics worried about our reputations rarely go. Moreover, even if Hicks's *Peaceable Kingdom* did not merit exile, any innocence we might experience in the composition—its freedom from intellectual wit and bravura and pictorial complexity, for instance, so like the freedom in Minimal sculpture and painting, and, for that matter, all great twentieth-century American art—has been robbed from us by that extremely calculated commercial genre called naïve painting. And, of course, the endless mimicry of Hicks's authentically naïve iconography into advertising for Bucks County getaway inns, suburban real estate, and autumn cozy-crafts festivals in small towns everywhere hasn't helped the artist, either. In the process of that appropriation, a great American artist had been deprived of his public, and we had lost him.

I have never been able to predict just when an oft-seen artwork will light up with abrupt new liveliness, insisting on revived attention—though such beautiful rebirth has been part of my experience of art since I began to write. In this case, however, the reason Hicks's *Peaceable Kingdom* did so surely had much to do with my recent thinking about England's peaceable kingdom in America. I did not know what to make of this historical epoch, or exactly what the documentary evidence I'd discovered (with the generous help of my cousin, Joe Chandler) was trying to tell me about my ancestors at the other end of American history.

This much was certain, at least about Hicks. The 1826 painting in Philadelphia is one of a hundred executed by the Pennsylvania sign painter and Quaker preacher between 1820 and his death in 1849, each entitled *The Peaceable Kingdom*. At the back of the Philadelphia work, the pioneering Quaker entrepreneur William Penn and the aboriginals are concluding an accord—probably Penn's "Great Treaty of 1682," entrenched in American folklore though probably fictitious—to establish a secure Quaker presence upon the North American continent. While presenting them as equal partners in this land deal, Hicks distinguishes the natives from the Quakers with numerous small touches. The aboriginals stir or sit beneath a pair of enormous trees, while the Europeans stand staunchly in full sunlight, with Penn at the center. The Englishmen's flat black hats and formal costumes contrast pointedly with the Indians' erect plumed headdresses and near-nakedness.

As portrayed in this serene vignette tucked into the back of Hicks's painting, the treaty is no trick to snatch native land away, no prelude to enslavement, but an affirmation of the peace that comes with liberty and equality. This last point is emphasized by the scene of wonderful animals in the foreground, feral and tame, lion and lamb, based on a brilliant passage about God's coming reign in the biblical prophecy of Isaiah. There is no crowding in the Peaceable Kingdom of Hicks's vision. He has accorded each animal such comfortable space and territory as its anatomy demands, even as he has given the natives and the Englishmen equal honor of place and space—all of it to express the artist's belief in the possibility of the peaceful reconciliation of opposites, both in this world and in the age to come.

Nothing in the Philadelphia picture points to the profound trouble shaking the soul of the remarkable artist who painted it, and who never stopped repainting the composition, for the rest of his days. Around 1820, Elias Hicks, Edward's kinsman and also a clergyman, launched a movement that plunged the American Quaker tradition into schism. The event agitated Edward deeply, and prompted the first *Peaceable Kingdom* étude—a counterstatement of hope, it appears, against the suffering that had divided Hicks's heart and his church.

From the long view, the American years around 1820 were not ones to inspire much pessimism about the present, or to send an artist off into a repetitious portrayal of a scene from the colonial period. The mood of the United States was bullish; the War of 1812 was past, and, with it, the menace of a return of British rule to America south of Canada. A generation after the Revolution, the bitter controversies over what sort of republic should be constructed were over, the Enlightenment theorists of America dead or too old to matter. The United States was secure, optimistic, and headed for a spectacular climax of its newfound mass-democratic consensus with the election of the back-country, anti-tidewater politician Andrew Jackson to the presidency in 1828. But art is often out of step with the popular culture of its time; and, surely, the American boosterism of his day interested Edward Hicks not at all. The new American Republic, as viewed from his Pennsylvania sign-painting shop, was an unhappy field, hectic with contentious Christian denominations and sects, loud revivalists, fire-breathing democratic politicians. What worried the artist most, however, was what he saw as the collapse of the old, deeply civilized Quaker ideal of *friendship* under the elephantine weight of America's industrial capitalism and frontier individualism. And for the last thirty years he lived, he replied to this general apostasy by painting and repainting his vision of the peace he believed Americans had forgotten, and the reign of fraternal covenant they had forfeited.

The content of that reply—the content of such rejoinders since the very birth of Western art and literature, through Rousseau to Lévi-Strauss—was a recollection of a Golden Age that could be restored if the citizenry had the courage to do so. The specific iconography of Hicks's prophecy was drawn from memories of the English colonial world. In declining to include important architecture or fast transportation or anything else that spoke to him of his fallen America, Hicks is presenting his country in its more virtuous dawn— primordial and innocent, at ease under the reign of treaty and covenant. Then, fields dappled with lights and shade were our floors, interlacing branches of trees the only roof we needed, the tall trunks of trees the only walls. Temples and fortresses had not arisen to enshroud our gods in darkness or keep out enemies, who had not, in any case, arisen to trouble us. A diffuse light brightens this idealized scene. Both the historical people in the background and the eschatological animals in the foreground are lit from within with the light that had broken forth within the first creation, and might, Hicks believed, again spring forth like a radiant fountain within the corrupted present.

But if put by the artist into an Edenic setting, Penn's accord with the American aborigines, Hicks well knew, did not take place in some very distant time. The peaceful culture of the late seventeenth and early eighteenth centuries lay outside living memory, but still not so far back to make it beyond reclamation. Viewed one way, the picture is among our earliest evidences for the unfolding mythology of the "Colonial" that, 150 years after the artist's death, still draws myriad Americans back to its shrines. But viewed from a more intimate perspective—the standpoint of another soul who had been alienated from a past, and who went to his ancestors' lands on the Appomattox River in an attempt to recall what was worthy in their culture and time—*The Peaceable Kingdom* spoke poignantly of the peaceful *American* kingdom that had prevailed in England's oldest continuing settlement of this land.

It was not hard to transpose John Maies and his sons into the place of Penn and his associates, and, replace the aborigines with John's partners in the orderly trade up and down the Virginia rivers. Nor was it difficult to see, in my mental reconstruction of Hicks's painting, a visible image of all that the numerous contracts and other documentary traces of my colonial family suggests: a Rousseauvian ellipsis of calm, sustained by a common economy of work and thought, and by the dependence of everyone on the fruitful earth. It was when visiting St. John's Church, and Westover, and, later, when perched on the muddy north side of the Appomattox, gazing across the sandbars and turbid flow at the bald, windswept penitentiary land where John Maies farmed, that I had first begun to understand, and sympathize with, the longings embedded in the cult of the "Colonial." But it was in Philadelphia that I came to understand why Hicks, and Americans ever since, have idealized the Colonial South, and sought nourishment there, when oppressed by the aggressive

City center, Hampton

culture of newer America's age of iron. Within the oldest English colony a civilization had arisen informed by an exemplary model of intelligent life: cosmopolitan, agrarian, and conventional, as all agrarian cultures are.

We cannot believe, of course, that colonial English Virginians were *better* folk than their Northern cousins, or anyone else, or that their culture was *really* a pure and ideal version of the Golden Age *redivivus*. It's nevertheless easy to understand why millions of Southerners, and other Americans, invest this era with sanctity worthy of pilgrimage and reverence. For during it, a certain memorable goodness blossomed on Southern land, destined to be forever called to mind whenever the churn of industrialization, the saturation of our lives by abstract technologies and the spectacle of mass communications, the uncontrollable concentration of crowds within cities, threaten America's primordial ideals of liberty.

PART TWO

REPUBLICAN VERSIONS

4

STRANGERS

Mountains, western Virginia

THE LAND WAS EVERYTHING. IN 1713, WHEN JOHN MAIES DIED, his tobacco plantations on the Appomattox River passed peacefully and completely to his elder son, Daniel, who did well there, and founded the impressive dynasty of resource-ful planters and merchants, ministers and lawyers from which my North Carolina cousin Joe is descended. Daniel's younger son, William, my ancestor, received not an acre; nor had he expected to. For in his day, and down to the early years of the republic, the ancient rule of primogeniture prevailed in Virginia, dictating the passage of valuables from father to first surviving son—serving to concentrate inherited wealth on one narrow genealogical avenue, and giving the notion of "honorable birth" a special emphasis that persisted among Southerners at least in Aunt Vandalia's day.

But William, a sensible and ambitious young man, had taken steps to ensure his future long before his father died. Knowing he stood to inherit nothing, he took the initiative one would expect of any young planter facing eventual landlessness, setting about acquiring his own properties and powers. William's rise to remarkable fortune began in 1690, when he was in his twenties, in real-estate partnership with his friend Henry Randolph II, offspring of one of the Virginia tidewater's most distinguished landowning families. And from the time of this start in business, with a plot of land near his father's plantation, the record of Virginia land sales and transfers is littered with young William's speculative purchases in and around his home parish of Bristol, and increasingly farther abroad in the Virginia countryside, where he sold and leased hundreds of acres to land-hungry new-comers. In the early years of the eighteenth century, he was busily enriching himself and his influential circle of friends and business partners at the comfortable center of English civilization, west of which—beyond the fall line—lay largely unknown wilderness.

William might have stayed rooted within the colony's center, had it not been for the appearance in the governor's mansion at Williamsburg, in 1727, of the enterprising figure of William Gooch. This energetic deputy of the Sovereign immediately set his hand to expanding the British presence in America, by opening it in the only direction it could go: west, inland, toward the mountains. The lure was land, which had long before proven its powers to draw men and women from the industrializing metropolitan centers of the British Isles to the outposts of empire.

By 1729 the first ships in the armada of northern Irish immigration encouraged by Governor Gooch and administrators in the other colonies had begun to arrive, and were catapulted inland from the ports by the old coastal settlers, who were jealous for both their land and the settled social and religious compacts of the sort to which John and his sons belonged.

The Scots-Irish had been officially welcomed, of course—or at least allowed to make landfall on the James River, in prelude to their setting out on the water roads beyond—because the King's ministers had decided the continental interior needed a fresh infusion of empire builders to safeguard British interests there. The newcomers—farmers and craftsmen, Presbyterians given to the hard work honored by their Calvinist confession—were certainly able to deliver that. But the tidewater authorities and high landowners had imported not independent eagles, but intrusive starlings, disinclined to deference toward the Anglican establishment headquartered at Williamsburg, and much inclined to belligerence toward anyone disagreeing with their sharply dogmatic Calvinism. Quaker planters went west beyond the fall line, and flourished there into the nineteenth century, despite fierce persecution by their Presbyterian neighbors for their pacifist convictions. Despite these conflicts, the southern Virginia piedmont was quickly, if sparsely, populated by this mostly contentious lot of newcomers—*colonized*, strictly speaking, but distinctly less *colonial* in matters of manner and traditional loyalties and temper. As they cut down the forests on the inland hills, and began to turn and plant the soil, they were turning the zone of their dwelling into a place apart—more a west-moving band of rough occupation than another delimited zone of New World civilization parceled up, in English fashion, into parishes. It was becoming the *frontier*, the site of a new American mind's emergence, and of a model of existence shaped by intolerance, and much tolerance for the isolation, hardship, and conflict with the resistant piedmont land.

Exactly why William Mayes, his wife and grown children, low-

country Anglicans with royal patents in hand, went west in the
1730s to claim their first four hundred acres is not known. It was
almost certainly not curiosity about an unknown land—the tidewater English colonials were not adventurous people—or destitution in
the fertile landscape they knew intimately. The reason, I suspect, was
business—the opportunity to invest and traffic in the new farmland
to which Gooch's advertisements, tax incentives, and other attractions were drawing immigrants from northern Ireland, and from the
northern American colonies. In any case, William Mays resettled on
the banks of the Staunton River in his middle years, and there my
ancestors lived until the eve of the Revolution.

The lay of the land, just east of the present-day village of
Brookneal, cleared by William and other racers in the land rush
Gooch had launched, would have surely seemed odd to my Mays
kin—and it *is* odd. Neither broadly open, like the tidewater, nor dramatic, as explorers had already found the Appalachian range to be,
the piedmont through which the Staunton flows is troubled,
uneven, mysterious in ways hard to pin down. Here, the rounded
ridges heave and drop steeply between deep, twisting, creek bottoms,
sliced deep and hard into the bedrock by fast water shed by the land.
Even the Staunton's wider waters, rushing toward the sea from the
Allegheny Mountains in present-day Montgomery County, lie deep
in their narrow bed, deeply shaded by the tangle and trees massed
on their narrow flood plain.

If I found the district strange, when driving its narrow roads and
stopping by creeks to listen to the water and the wind riffling the
treetops far overhead, I was to find later that this landscape had long
bred strange memories, as twisted and dark as the gullies in the
ground. The name by which the region's principal river is known—
which local people pronounce as though it were spelled *Stanton*—is
one such curiosity; for it rises in the mountains and concludes at the
Atlantic as the Roanoke, taking on the name *Staunton* only in its
winding run across this part of southern Virginia. Another curiosity
is the origin of the name. People in that district tell a story of one
Captain Henry Staunton, later a warrior in the Revolution, though
in William's day a defender of settlers from the hostile aboriginal
tribes still roaming the forest beyond the tobacco fields. It is said that,
during this stint, Captain Staunton rescued a young woman who had

been taken captive by the natives, making good his escape by carrying the girl down the riverbed, thereby hiding his tracks, and getting a river named after him in the bargain. It is a story that cannot be true. The diarist William Byrd of Westover had called this waterway the "Stanton" in 1728, before settlers needing military protection had populated those hills, before English girls were there to be spirited away, or valiant officers to rescue them. So there remains a mystery about the name, which the river keeps to itself, and will probably keep until people stop wanting certainties about such matters.

Of the land traversed by Staunton waters, the legends told have a similar shadow of myth about them. A chronicler who dwelt there some years ago wrote down a description of the district, as she experienced it in life, tradition, and story: a wasteland canopied by immense trees, casting a shadow so deep that "neither grass could grow nor seed develop to feed wild animals and game birds; even our familiar song birds were absent." In so peculiar and desolate a place, we should not find it remarkable that the earliest settlers found themselves "strangers in a strange land, oppressed with the silence and loneliness of the great forest all about them, and ever watchful and dreaded the expected attack of the Red Man." In this narrative, the hill country becomes a land beyond history, even beyond Nature as we know it, busy with animals and birds—a dark quiet spot somewhere far back in deep time, that we denizens of a newer age can visit only in the oldest stories.

But the land along the Staunton has never been the sort of place that allows many memories to survive unwarped or unerased, for very long anyway. If the earliest white settlers there left monuments to mark the burial places of their dead, the stones were long ago swallowed up by the green gloom; the bones of William and his son Mattox, my ancestor, together with their kinsmen and neighbors, lie in unknown, unattended graves. Of William's dwelling place, and that of his son on Mays Creek—"where I live," Mattox states in his will of 1773—no memory remains. The name *Mays Creek* itself has vanished from the map, and from local recollection. The very existence of the Mays planters who had opened and eventually cultivated hundreds of acres on those hills had fallen from the region's story by 1850, when William Irvin, descendant of an early planter, wrote: "And it certainly is a fact that this place"—the land granted his ancestor around 1735, the year my ancestor William received his, in the same vicinity—was "the first plantation that was ever settled and cultivated within 35 or 40 miles of the same."

If Irvin's 1850 writing takes us only to a shut door on the tenure of William and Mattox Mays, it opens another, intriguing one. Through it we glimpse a man—or, rather, the ancient figure of a man—who had been drifting through the shadowy corridors of family memory long before Irvin sat down to write, and who lives on—I learned this from Edith Poindexter of Brookneal, a keeper of the region's memories—in tales twice-told along the Staunton to this day.

When his Irish-born grandfather, John Irvin, arrived from Pennsylvania in the 1730s to claim his Crown grant in timbered wilderness near the Staunton, writes the grandson, he was greeted by an old man living on the land he had been granted—"an individual white man only, and he just ready to die; and no one living in many miles of the place." This man of the forest told John that he was glad for him to "take possession here on promise of grandfather that he was to remain here what little time he was to live and be attended to." Having decided on the site and situation of the house he would build, John Irvin returned to Pennsylvania to collect his family and slaves, and move them to Virginia. And when he returned, in 1736, he found the old man still alive and living on his property. Not long after, his elderly tenant died, "and lies by the side of a large rock at this upper end of a field next to Little Falling River."

The story has inspired quests at the "large rock" (which is said to be there today on Little Falling River) for a hint where his grave might be—all to no avail. But why? Why the seeking and searching, and the stubborn remembering of *this* story? On the face of it, it seems plausible, and complete enough. A new farming family comes to take possession of their gift of land, only to find an older settler living on it, who never bothered to lay formal, legal claim to the property. But being kindhearted folk, the young couple allows him to stay—in cabin or lean-to—until the end of his days, then fast approaching. Such collisions almost certainly did happen later in the eighteenth century, if only because the land-starved were scattering westward faster and more haphazardly than the orderly paperwork of land-granting could keep up with. If his family memory is true, in any case, John Irvin was not outraged to find an occupant on the land he'd acquired, and hardly unwilling to oblige his unexpected tenant.

But when I first heard it, I sensed something more to the story than that—an unmistakable aroma of deeper mystery, and an oddity that kept it circling the far edges of my mind for weeks. This strangeness seems to arise, at least in part, from its improbability. As we have seen, the darkly forested, creek-riven hill country along the Staunton has long been thought to be extraordinarily forbidding, even to wild animals and the Virginia's lovely songbirds—at least until the oncoming of English settlers, with ax and adze and gun. What would "an individual white man only" have been doing in so dangerous and exposed a place, *before* the arrival of order and civilization?

Peering around the corner of the time-smoothed façade of William Irvin's nineteenth-century retelling, we catch sight of a man who seems, not merely *old*, but *primordial*—at home, as civilized people are not, in isolated groves and gullies, and among the bears and wolves and aboriginal peoples that infested the fantasies of America's first English settlers. As we discover often, upon opening one of those modest ragbags of local legend and anecdote often found, and largely ignored, at historic sites and shrines across America, ancient lights glimmer in the most ordinary stories told over generations. We recognize the old man on the Staunton, *the outsider,* only because we have met him so many times before in the West's great literature and art—in the self-portrayals of the Beat poets, novelists, and artists as wild men and outlaws, outside *our* laws, for example; in Conrad and Dostoyevsky and in the characters of both Caliban and Ariel in *The Tempest*. We have met him in the medieval epics of chivalry, where the old man appears in the guise of monk or hermit, emerging from mystery and tangled forest gloom into civilization's clearing when it suits his magical purpose, then disappearing back into it; and even in our nursery tales of fauns and satyrs and sylphs, and in Grimm.

But one recognizes the old man John Irvin encountered quickest of all, if one has already met the Wild Folk. As the large library of words and images from ancient through medieval times tells us, humans *older* than the civilized townspeople and farmers had lived forever in the great European forests. They were shaggy, their hair matted with filth; and they had no language. They either hated God, like Caliban, or did not know Him, and gobbled down their kills raw and whole. They enjoyed principally two kinds of relationships among themselves and other people: quick, animal coupling, or mutual bashing with a wooden stump.

But that was how they behaved in the oldest versions of their story. By the dawn of the Renaissance, the Wild People had remarkably improved. They were still children of the forest, but no longer hostile and dirty. They roamed early Modern Europe's shrinking woodlands as gentle survivors of the Golden Age lying far behind the dark medieval centuries, embodying goodness and freedom *sans* civilization, hence *sans* vice: the Beats become canonical in the literature departments, the outsiders become *almost* insiders in the grand assimilating churn of our Modern culture. It is the Wild Man, as re-created by this newer imagination, who steps forward to greet John Irvin in his descendant's tale. He is dying; like the North American aborginals he *must* die, for the primeval forest itself—his home, his source, the ground of his identity—must vanish, to make way for tobacco fields and to provide materials for houses and bridges and barns. Here is the classic Modern encounter between men from the two great orders of time, the Old and the New: forest hermit and civilizing knight; or a frail Titan, and young, vigorous Olympians come to claim the land they won from the older order. Here, too, is the old man's assertion of forest rights more ancient and more binding than the ones known to modern kings and their lawyers and grant-givers; and the voluntary relinquishment of those rights—but on condition that he be cared for until death, and buried near a great stone, from highest antiquity to the present the West's most resonant symbol of what is ancient, what endures and is immortal.

Lingering in the background of the narrative, however, is the faintest threat of *curse*—some unnamed misery that would befall John and Mary Irvin if they did *not* assent to the old man's request. It may have been the curse of being forgotten, which the Irvins were not, and are not, in southern Virginia down to this day. As it stands, this haunting legend, of course, does not explain why my Mays ancestors, who came to this district at the same time as the Irvins, have been lost to local memory. But when beating a way through underbrush crowding thick against a fast, narrow stream that might have been Mays Creek, allowing my imagination to take me farther than knowledge could, I wondered whether my ancestors' disappearance from local story was sealed by meeting the same old man of the wild wood, hearing him out—but denying this dying Titan his grave on their newly squared-off turf.

Be that as it may, the rational opening of farmland by my Mays forbears, and many others, along the Staunton ended long ago; and the forest has returned to claim the wild ground. In my search for evidence of my family's passages over the American land, I had never found the record more barren, the references scantier, than *here,* in their inner Virginia years, between the 1730s and the Revolution. Indeed, in all my travels in search of the dwelling places, I had never discovered a place less welcoming to any footfall, let alone habitation, or more closely guarded by the hostile spirits who preside over spots once dwelt upon, then abandoned. Up the hills from the larger streams emptying into the Staunton, a new wilderness of second growth, coarse and tangled and trackless, has taken possession— the old man's ancient wildness returning to reclaim the land.

One spring afternoon, when gathering wildflowers not far from Brookneal, on the hard, damp bank of Catawba Creek, which flows into the Staunton—something I try to do wherever I travel, just to relieve the taupe dullness of universal Motel Room decor—I felt the *genius loci* of the Staunton, the true owner of these hills and streams, standing near, watching, not too far away.

I was gathering *his* violets. An interloper might be allowed to pick them, though not many, and not for long; then the visitor had best be on his way. The spirit, I decided, is one of those who is neither good nor evil, but who delights in dark extremes. He has never wanted people cluttering up his dark silence and emptiness—least of all folk like William and Mattox Mays, attracted west into *his* wilds by the profane, ordinary motives of good investment from the civilized Anglican *imperium* lying east, on the James and Chesapeake Bay. If people had to come to his woodlands, let them be *ideologues* like the Scots-Irish Presbyterians—permanently restless, inclined to sectarian fanaticism and hatred of Quakers, Anglicans, and Roman Catholics alike, ready to make trouble for anyone opposed to their version of the democracy of God on earth, ready to move on and leave the spirit's woods empty again.

My Anglican ancestors were certainly not the contentious, sectarian, mobile people the Staunton's wild spirit wanted, and he made a swift end to their tenuous hold on his territory. In 1747, scarcely more than a decade after receiving his land upriver, William Mays considered his end and made his will, and died four years later. If he had dreams of establishing grand plantations on the Staunton, they never came true. William left little more to his eldest son than he had when he arrived: "the plantation he lives on, and all the land belonging on the upper side of Hat Creek being part of 400 acres," and another plantation on the Staunton. To daughter Frances, he gave property on the river, though with an odd stipulation designed to keep her from using it—an abrogation of the gift, should she or her husband "leave, rent, destroy or sell any timber." Lucy got hogs, a valuable gift. William's younger son Joseph was accorded "3 Indian slaves," and Mattox—my last Mays ancestor to live and leave his life in royal America—received one.

He probably needed nothing more. Like his father a younger son with ambition, Mattox always knew he stood to inherit no land. And, surely, had his father stayed in the vicinity of his Appomattox River homeplace, he would have found very little land to acquire; by 1720, when Mattox was ten years old, the accumulation by other speculators of all the arable ground and pasturage on the coastal plain and lowlands was complete. So it was that young Mattox took up business on the Staunton, and there followed his father's example set on the Appomattox, drawing together, trading, and acquiring land. He was to die beside Staunton waters; whether he actually moved there at once after receiving his first grant of Crown land in 1736, or brokered his newfound land from the relative comfort of his old home terrain, I do not know. But over the first decade following his grant, Mattox, still unmarried, put together by purchase or grant a handsome cluster of plantations covering more than fifteen hundred acres, scattered along creeks south of Staunton—then began, almost immediately, to sell it off bit by bit in the game of land speculation at which his downriver Mays relations and ancestors had enriched themselves. His holdings increased again after his financially prudent marriage, in the 1750s and his own late middle age, to Dorcas Abney, a young neighbor and scion of a plantation family as deeply rooted in Virginia soil and history as his own.

By the 1770s his vicinity was rapidly filling up with men and women who needed the land he had to sell, and found in him a ready seller. Mattox had witnessed the opening of wagon roads where only trails through the forest had been; and, with the roads, the opening of overland rivers for his wagonloads of tobacco and wheat, rumbling down to the fall-line markets on tracks rutted by the hooves of cattle and swine. And he had lived to witness the paradoxical overture typical of every outbreak of colonial revolution: the abrupt upsurge of Virginia's economy within the British imperial system brought on by expanding markets for corn and wheat in southern Europe, the West Indies, and Britain's more northerly colonies on the American continent. Coming to the end of his life in 1773, "being weak in body but of sound & perfect memory," as he tells us in his will, Mattox had accomplished perhaps as much as any man in his time and in that hostile inland district could.

The *genius* of the Staunton had spared Mattox, allowing my ancestor to pick the fruit of his hills for almost forty years. But the invoice for this tolerance was to go not to Mattox, but to his widow, Dorcas Abney. She had borne her husband three sons and two daughters in quick succession, and was still young when he died— and the combination of youth, a platoon of small children, and no husband could hardly have been more tolerable to a woman two centuries ago than it is now. And the will was—inadvertently, I assume—treacherous. Dorcas had been left black slaves to do the work—Captain, Pompey, Jude, Frank, Luna, Sal, Dafney, Jutah, and Bob are named in the will—but no son old enough to assume responsibility for overseeing the plantations Mattox had bequeathed her. And when her first son, my ancestor Abney, reached majority— so her husband's will decreed—the lands were to be "equally divided amongst all my then surviving children, shear and shear alike allowing my eldest son choice . . . provided that my well-beloved wife Dorcas Mays be allowed her first choice in the land as tenant for life." If this sounds like a prescription for strife, it almost certainly was; and Dorcas knew it. As soon after Mattox's death as she could decently do so, Dorcas wed her neighbor, family friend, and contemporary William Hill, who had stood by Mattox's bed steadying the dying man's hand while he signed his final testament, and adding his own as witness.

William Hill was not only a good thirty years younger than the
husband he replaced; he was also a man different from the Mayses
who had preceded him into Staunton River country. Both William
Mays and his son Mattox had been heirs of coastal colonial convictions—royalist, Anglican, conventional. While their goal in moving
their business interests west was financial gain, they certainly imagined no radical break from the culture they had left behind, but
rather the reproduction, more or less intact, of the rural peaceable
kingdom enjoyed by their ancestors from the middle years of the
seventeenth century onward. On the cultural side, they appear to
have been successful, stitching themselves and their families into
other families of the old colonial patriarchy similarly displaced westward. But their success was short-lived, and superficial. The symbols
of English dominion were being steadily weakened by distance, and
by the spiritual difference between the inland and coastal topogra-
phies. By the 1770s on Mays Creek, the pre-Revolutionary quarrels
at Williamsburg must have seemed far away—as far away as the
Anglican Church, which rarely sent its ministers into that hostile
Presbyterian county—and largely irrelevant to everyday toil and custom, which were carried on at the American frontier according to old
methods learned in the English colony. By that time, as well, allegiance to the Hanoverian on his throne in London must have been
little more than a perfunctory formality—though observed by my
Mays ancestors in the way most people observe old traditions, the
origins of which they've forgotten, merely because the traditions are
there, and a part of one's existence in a place. From the beginning of
his adult life and western career, Mattox lived in an abruptly more
fractured mental world than did his easterly kin in the colony. Yet he
had persisted in the old ways, as he understood them, and prospered.

For Dorcas's new husband, however, the great break with all that,
shortly to divide colonist against colonist in America, had already
taken place in his soul. He was a Scots-Irishman born in the rough
Virginia upcountry, and a native to its culture of sharp religious and
political dissent and discussion—a man no less enterprising than the
Mayses, but driven by a hankering for new, free farmland to plow
and tend even farther inland from sophisticated Williamsburg. It was
such aspiration that caused him to pack up his belongings, and load

his new family into a wagon, and set out southward, within months of Mattox's death. After the British invasion of South Carolina in 1780, he would fight briefly on the republican side before getting back to his chosen work of clearing and farming and providing for Dorcas, his stepchildren, and his son by Dorcas, Dannett Hill. But in Virginia, as late as 1775, he was still something of a true King's man—true enough, in any case, to think it no contradiction to take up the King's offer of free land in the unruly hinterland of western South Carolina, then join the river of Quakers and Calvinists, Germans and Scots-Irish, and other Englishmen flowing down the Great Wagon Road south through the Shenandoah Valley, just before helping drive old George and his viceroys and loyal subjects out forever.

Another troupe of intruders gone! the wild Staunton spirit said to himself, when the wagons carrying the Hills and the Mays children rattled off into the distance. And, indeed, on the eve of the Revolution, within only a few decades of the first influx of settlers, the region transected by the Staunton River would be almost as empty of people as it was before the immigration began. But that renewed emptiness attracted a few people with the blazing tempers and hatred of the old established order in Virginia the genius loci loved, and who, in turn, found the strict angel of the place attractive company.

The most famous of them all was Patrick Henry. Twice more elected governor of republican Virginia after his inaugural term, despised by Thomas Jefferson and other Revolutionary aristocrats as a rabble-rousing demagogue, and still adored by the hardscrabble farmers and small upcountry landowners of piedmont Virginia as their true son, Henry exchanged his flamboyant public career for retirement at remote Long Island, in the Staunton valley, in 1792. Two years later, he bought Red Hill plantation and the little homestead house on it, some eighteen miles downriver from Long Island and very near the first tract granted William Mayes a half-century before.

In turning the story to Patrick Henry at this point, I am not abandoning my family. But, for now, the young sons and daughters of Mattox Mays need time to find their way to a new homeland in South Carolina, to grow into the men and women they will be when we rejoin them. Too, pausing in Virginia awhile longer, as my ancestors' wagons rattle away in the direction of the nineteenth century, provides a chance to consider a version of the young American Republic—Patrick Henry's influential interpretation—that those children and their Mays descendants down to Aunt Vandalia's generation rejected in favor of another.

For some time before his move to Red Hill, Henry had been seeking refuge from public life and its politics and business, and, in the plantation's sternly plain frame house, had found it. According to a storyteller in that district, the river valley was "wild and desolate" when Henry "turned his back upon the world, and entered this beautiful wilderness that stretched eastward from the Peaks of Otter. A few Indians were there, and many bears. . . ." That rugged topography suited him very well. He called it "the garden spot of the world," and, writes the same local historian, "he loved to watch growing crops, and to wander over his broad fields . . . He would stand on the hill and scan the river with his spy glass, watching for the approach of his boats. The great voice which cried, 'If this be treason, make the most of it!' could be heard shouting directions from his front lawn to the hands in the low grounds. . . ."

In the five years of life remaining to him—Henry died in 1799—the elderly fanatic turned his energies, with characteristic obsession, to the new project of securing large estates for his several sons, which he did. The success of these last years in Red Hill was largely accidental, as it happened, because the man's remarkable mind was cleverest when inflamed by fantasies of vengeance and paradise, and merely routine when the matters at hand involved dull legalities and the practice of law he was trained in. Nearing the end of his days, "Henry had a speculator's desire but a householder's mentality," Henry Mayer has written in a recent biography. "His social vision remained the utopian hope of the Revolution that yeomen would find contentment under their vines and fig trees; that is how he chose to end his days, and that is what he wanted for his sons." He was put into a grave at Red Hill, which remained unmarked until a son put on it a plain stone—not in tribute, it appears, but as gentle frustration to post-Revolutionary idolaters who wished to exhume the body and translate his relics to a massive tomb proposed for Richmond. The strategy worked; Henry's earthly remains were kept far from Virginia's gracious state capitol building, designed by

Henry's old enemy Thomas Jefferson in homage to the Maison Carré, a beautiful Roman temple still standing in Nîmes, and to the Classical ideals of equilibrium and refinement that Henry hated; and the old radical's earthly remains rest beside the Staunton River today.

What struck me most urgently about the house I found on the open, sloping riverside property overseen by the Patrick Henry Memorial Foundation was its incongruity. Pensioned-off politicians, especially very famous ones like Henry, customarily install themselves in houses befitting their status: Jefferson's Monticello, for example, which bankrupted its owner and architect, but did leave us, as he intended, an extraordinary expression of high Enlightenment convictions. The house at Red Hill is a similarly conscious declaration of cultural values—though Henry, then one of the wealthiest landowners in the fledgling United States, chose for *his* expression the plain dwelling of a small farmer. It did not stand that way for long, by the way. Patrick's son John dignified it with a two-story addition. Then, in 1910, with the zeal typical of the patriotic progeny of conspicuous American revolutionaries, a descendant hired the Philadelphia architect Charles Barton Keane to elaborate the original shelter in ways she considered fitting for so powerful an ancestral memory, by inflating it into a grandiose eighteen-room mansion.

By 1919, when all was destroyed by fire, almost every trace of what Red Hill house had been or looked like had been similarly swept away by forgetfulness, except for some drawings and personal remembrances of the Lynchburg architect Stanhope Johnson, Keane's assistant on the 1910 expansion. They were to prove precious legacies to Henry enthusiasts in the 1950s, when a project of reconstruction was undertaken on behalf of patriotic neighbors and wealthy patrons. Johnson's re-creation is remarkable for its time, inasmuch as Johnson rejected the "Colonial" preservationist fantasies favored in America since the redoing of Williamsburg in the 1930s, and showed his loyalty to archaeological realism. He sought to realize the truest replica he could imagine of the house that once rose from the remaining foundations—innocent of ornament or archaic flourish, sternly loyal to its structural engineering.

Like Westover in its way and like any other built object—Red Hill's architectural forms and details are encoded with signs leading outward, into the forest of opinions and beliefs from which the actual timber of building was extracted. The house was built by stubborn immigrants who had homesteaded on the Staunton long before Henry bought his last country seat there. If Johnson has his reconstruction right, the appeal of the severe original for Henry surely lay in its recalling of this frontier rudeness, of the plain, simple lives lived far from the sophisticated metropolitan centers of the new republic, and the stern greatness of Rome. But such primitivism—the reinvention of Classical antiquity's agrarian dignity and simplicity on American soil—was very much alive everywhere in the air of the early republic. What mattered was which version of rural primitivism one fabricated from the multifarious field of Roman history, the common source favored by all parties.

For Jefferson, the favored model was drawn from the imperial Roman Republic of Augustus, and of Virgil, the gentleman-farmer, brilliant poet, genealogist. Jefferson's learned intellectual and architectural tastes were among the things Henry had against him; for Augustan Rome was already too late, too decadent for the old firebrand of the Staunton. Henry admired the earlier, sterner republic of rough farmers, thrifty and practical, independent, and rooted firmly on their small plots of land.

And so it was that the great Jacobin of the American Revolution lived out his days in a house free of arch or architrave, pediment and entablature, columns and dome—architectural embellishments magnificently optimistic to the mind of Thomas Jefferson, deeply objectionable to Henry's. The model house he had found beside the Staunton River was a primitive hut that spoke of honest simplicity, even as the eastern Virginia mansions spoke, to him anyway, of pretension. So it was, not for lack of money or power or prestige, but from the sincere ideological advocacy of primitive democracy, and as resistance to the seductive autocratic elegance he hated and feared, that Patrick Henry shoehorned his large family into the impossibly small, rude old house at Red Hill, and lived there until he died.

Henry may, or may not, have heard of the Old Man from his Irvin neighbors. It would be interesting to know if he had learned the family legend, the incidents it preserved already long past by the time he came to the valley, and what he thought of it. But never mind. Surely without recognizing he was doing so, Henry had *become*

William Irvin's Old Man, "an individual white man only, and he just
ready to die." Wandering over the grounds well-kept by the Henry
foundation, I again felt the nearness of the *genius loci*, peering from
the nearby forest darkness; and was reminded, a second time, of
whose lawns I trod, and the brevity of my permission to tread them.
The spirit knows his own—he always has—and drew the early
republic's most celebrated loner and dissenter to his hills and ravines,
to live out the last years of a famous life, and to die.

If I was not one of those souls destined to stay long on the Staunton,
the son of Mattox Mays was not one, either. Nor, to my knowledge,
have any of the Mays families descended from Daniel and William in
seventeenth-century Virginia had a taste for the radical populism at
the heart of Henry's proposal for the American Republic. His version
sprang from a certain experience of the South during the eighteenth
century—from an extreme idealism that arose from hard pioneering
in the upcountry, from the fierce individualism of the Scots-Irish folk
who triumphed over the forest dark of the continental interior. Such
idealism, I believe, lies at the root of the South's besetting sin, radical
sentimentality—a discontent with rigorous thought in matters of politics and religion, a poisonous hankering for the way things "used to
be," as they appear in half-understood and heavily edited recollections of the past. We Southerners have known where such individu-
alistic sentimentality can lead: to irrational, right-wing Christian
piety, to the deranged clinging to the past that precipitated our dev-
astating rebellion against the United States in 1861, and to the season of rage and terror that followed military defeat in 1865, and
then, a century later, to hateful resistance against the extension of
full civil rights to all Southerners. Inspiring all these bloody tumults
has been the inexpressibly sweet, mad-making Southern liquor of
revolutionary sentiment, its recipe written long ago by radical patriots such as Patrick Henry, and distilled in the violent kitchens of the
Southern upcountry.

   While a man of the South, Henry was not a *Southerner*, at least as
that word gradually came to be understood in the decades leading up
to 1861, and is popularly understood today—imbued with Stoic resignation, an abiding preference for Augustan order and balance, and
a belief in the Southern land as the source of self-understanding and

destiny, and disinclined to extremism of any sort. As I have argued earlier in this book, such a definition of Southern identity is doomed by its simplism, inasmuch as it fails to comprehend the contradiction and complexity of the Southern experience. But it is not wholly false. And even as this autocratic, Virgilian ideal prevailed as an unwritten code in my family for many decades after the Revolution—and it prevailed powerfully there—it has never disappeared from my own dreams and best hopes for the South.

But no Southerner, I suspect, can expect to be wholly free of the temptation to the opposite, radical sentimentality lying in the deep wells of our regional imagination. I have tasted it, and gotten drunk on it at least twice. On the first occasion, in my early twenties—in a passage of life I have written of already—I tried to force myself into rigid, dead antiquarianism as a substitute for the plantation childhood I had lost. On the second, later in the same decade of my life, toward the end of my descent into mental ruin, I attempted to slash the ties that bound me to those malignant certainties—to forget the South and its traditions, and the imperatives written in the history of my family—to forget what I could not forget, which was myself.

In my last days of roaming the back roads and the tight, small creeks of the Roanoke Valley district, I found myself thinking often of the Southern extremism nurtured during more than two centuries in that strange hill country—not in the abstract, or as some historical phenomenon I knew only at arm's length, but as the source of my own intoxications. And I thought often, as well, of the years of healing that followed the most intense seasons of mental darkness—what had spoken to my soul then, and helped its mending.

I traveled widely in those days, often to the loneliest edges of continents, to walk and think and read in the peace I could not find closer to home. But of all the far coasts I found refuge on, none meant more to me than the rocky, bare Irish islands off Galway. Celtic Christian saints had been there fifteen centuries before, refugees from the madness of a world disintegrating. It was in Virginia that I began thinking again—after many years of deliberately *not* giving much thought to it—about that hard passage in my life, and a particular moment of it in Ireland.

I remembered the sound of cold rain dashing against the wind-clattered window as I sat close to the peat fire, the Atlantic howl battering the stone cottage on the island of Aranmor, off Ireland's west coast, in the spring of 1970. By that time, I had been largely incapacitated for almost two years, able to teach only a little, and to write not at all. In the belief they might do me good, I had come to that western Irish island for long hikes along its high cliff edge—only to have the storm immediately confine me to the cottage hearth. I had brought along a few books, as I always do, to fill the hours when travel becomes stalled, or stale, as it almost always does, and the sudden descent of vicious weather made me glad for their companionship. I had no prior commitment to read any of them, or to read them *then*, anyway. But I would certainly have gotten around to Lévi-Strauss's *Tristes Tropiques* eventually—it was one of those books I tucked into my baggage—if only because Susan Sontag had included a piece on it in *Against Interpretation*.

In the last days of light before my nervous breakdown, in 1968, I had adopted Sontag's collection of brilliant reviews and essays as a syllabus of books, films, plays, prose, and creative minds I wanted to know. Only recently out of the small-town South—and with precious little experience of the world outside books, cinemas, and seminar rooms—I needed such a book list. Before I reached Ireland's western islands, I had made my first sightings of America's advanced contemporary art, and taken the first steps into the intellectual worlds of Modern European writers, such as Genet and Ionesco and Nathalie Sarraute, and filmmakers including Robert Bresson and Alain Resnais and Jean-Luc Godard—then gone beyond, into the larger worlds of late Modern art from which such creators drew their imaginative forms. If today the creative landscape gazetteered in *Against Interpretation* seems less fascinating than it once did, and the writers more old-fashioned, the handbook had the good effect of turning me toward sensibilities of Modern alienation and Modern loss I might never have otherwise encountered.

I do not now recall just why I brought along the book on that voyage. But picking up Sontag's essay on *Tristes Tropiques* twenty-five years after Ireland, I find the choice unmysterious.

"Most serious thought in our time struggles with the feeling of homelessness," Sontag writes in *Against Interpretation*. "The felt unreliability of human experience brought about by the inhuman acceleration of historical change has led every sensitive modern mind to the recording of some kind of nausea, of intellectual vertigo, and the only way to cure this spiritual nausea seems to be, at least initially, to exacerbate it."

In Sontag's view, Lévi-Strauss earned his spurs as a hero of the Modern condition by turning general existential homelessness—Modernity's affliction and trademark—into an all-absorbing career in the realms of the Exotic and the Other, pursued with "spiritual commitment like that of the creative artist or the adventurer or the psychoanalyst."

By the time the storm broke over the Irish island, and I got around to reading *Tristes Tropiques*, I found in it a patient, deeply intelligent inquirer, but little in the book that spoke to me of *heroism*. Underneath Sontag's solemnity, her observation about the tendency of the "sensitive modern mind" to embrace rootlessness, rather than escape this condition, is shrewd. But the notion that voluntary, ascetic, and unrelenting alienation—negotiating self-imposed *strangeness* as a gesture of opposition to mass cultural leveling—was sounding a bit shrill and more than a bit false. I had learned, after all, that I was not one of Nietzsche's "great despisers . . . venerators and arrows of yearning toward the other shore"—but a seeker for home, and for moorings sunk in less cerebral sand.

Long-damped longings had begun to stir in me before I went to Ireland, and now they began to glow faintly, like the peat embers in the grate, illuminating something within me that I could not make out by their pale light. So I impatiently picked up the other book on Sontag's syllabus I'd slipped into my bags, and read until the storm's onslaught lightened enough to make possible the long walks on the Irish sea cliffs.

Though I'd begun it several times before, this was the first time I finished Simone Weil's *The Need for Roots*. The book was given to me in 1968 by an Episcopalian priest and friend during a bright spell between mental batterings. At the outset, I found in its French author a spiritual sister, an outsider to the same ordinary grace from which I felt exiled by depression. Yet I soon realized our kinship was mistaken fantasy on my part. For at some level I believed I would survive my disorder, and find my place in the disordered world, as she did not. Dying in London in early 1943, Weil wrote the book on commission from de Gaulle, as a plan for the postwar reconstruction of France. The General apparently intended the job as patriotic busy-work to occupy this strange, frail creature who kept turning up at Free French headquarters, insisting on being parachuted into occu-pied territory to join the *Résistance*. Instead of a practical plan, how-ever, Weil produced a radical meditation on belonging and duty, uprooting and putting down roots—on what she calls "the needs of the soul."

De Gaulle's response to the report is unknown; he probably never saw it. It was not published until 1949. And while musings on root-lessness and groundless dread were stylish among influential Parisian intellectuals around 1950, nobody appears to have paid much atten-tion to this French Jew perhaps *too* deeply in love with Christ and the Roman Catholic Church. And as for the powerful and well-positioned remakers of the war-ruined continent—their minds were fixed on earthly matters. The book turned out to be one of those that "do not influence the contemporary conduct of affairs," T. S. Eliot writes in his preface to the English translation. "[F]or the men and women already engaged in this career and committed to the jargon of the market place, they always come too late." Eliot was right; and *The Need for Roots* has long enjoyed a odd reputation as one of Mod-ern thought's most interesting wrecks, and one of its most assidu-ously unread accomplishments.

Weil believed that the longing for grounding is a *basic, undeniable need*, like sex and sleep—a proposition I found hard to admit at the time of my trip to Ireland, because I had almost convinced myself to stop trying to find a place to put down roots. She also maintained that, because this need is radical to our nature, it cannot be an object of suspicion or shame; nor can the quest for roots be undertaken in solitude. "A human being has roots by virtue of his real, active, and natural participation in the life of a community, which preserves in living shape certain particular treasures of the past and certain par-ticular expectations for the future . . . It is necessary for him to draw well-nigh the whole of his moral, intellectual, and spiritual life [from] the environment of which he forms a natural part." Had Weil not died shortly after finishing her book, this woman of extremes might have turned from the polemicist of *The Need for Roots* into a mourner for the old, high-cultural Europe that she belonged to, and that fascism and war had mostly destroyed, with postwar developers, speculators, and politicians bulldozing what was left. Death spared her the fate of the seer Cassandra, whose prophecies, however true, were doomed never to be believed.

Dying young saved Simone Weil from another unhappiness: the intensified difficulty of seeking roots in our mass culture, which she did not live to see—the flux of television and advertising images, disintegrating moral authority, distracting spectacles and pomps, the withdrawal of millions from the project of civilization into isolated fancies. Is it strange that her essential summons to partake in that great project rings with a harsh clang today? As I was finding, the need for roots in an unreal time can only be satisfied by embracing reality—in my case, and during my own attempt to acknowledge the South in myself, the embrace of the South as it was and is: conflicted and complex, shot through with contradiction.

The South, after all, is the sum of its pluralities; and one of these is liberty. The stark individualism and extreme freedom from precedent so passionately cherished by Patrick Henry and the Scots-Irish settlers of the mid-eighteenth century is one version of America that springs from the Southern earth; but it is not the liberty of the Mays families of the South, nor is it mine. In the blood of few descendants of the Puritan minister at Kecoughtan, and none of my ancestors, has ever flowed radical fire, or much militancy. No man in my Mays line took part in the various revolts and civil tumults that shook the early Virginia colony from time to time; nor did any take up arms in the Revolutionary wars, or in the sporadic outbreaks of anti-Tory terror that accompanied them in the Virginia and South Carolina upcountry. Though my great-grandfather John, after his rise to wealth and position in east Texas, liked to wreathe his Civil War record with fashionable valor, he served the Rebellion only a short while, as a lookout on the Savannah River. Neither my grandfather nor my father fought in any war.

While the dispersed Mays families of the South—as opposed to the Mayses, here and there, like me—have not been Episcopalian in name since the Revolution, and usually Methodist or Presbyterian or nothing in particular, we have very largely tended to keep to the old Anglican *via media* between extremes, shoring up the temperate liberty in whatever American civilization we have found ourselves, Colonial or Republican or Secessionist or Reconstructionist. Our

Abandoned house, North Carolina

Southern freedom has been exercised, not in flamboyant rhetoric, but the founding of towns and banks and stores, teaching school and practicing law and serving in legislative assemblies, and governing the institutions that hold us within the fragile bounds of order. Through the first seven generations, most of us earned our livelihoods from Southern land extending from the Carolina and Virginia coasts to the red hills of Louisiana. If we men and women of the eighth generation, and our descendants in the ninth and tenth no longer do so, we have always tended to sustain civilized order, in teaching and writing, the courts and the mainline churches, even as the orderly seasons on the land sustained us over the early centuries of our tenure.

But I love the wilds and deeps of those Virginia hills along the Staunton near Brookneal, while knowing I am not a man who belongs to them. Nor has the longing to travel on the world's lonely edges, to dwell in radical emptiness outside the complexities of the current age awhile, ever left me. Little in the system of modern institutions and modern cares and matters can hold one's attention for long, and much in that system distracts us from essential thinking. And even now, from time to time—when least expecting it to happen—I find the emptiness drawing near, calling me into its peculiar quiet. The summons can come anytime, anyplace: in a desolate urban prairie pocked by the hulks of rotting factories, from a street unaccountably empty at noonday.

5

CINCINNATUS

Store, near Spring Ridge

THE MUDDY RUT OF THE GREAT WAGON ROAD WAS GASHED ON the Atlantic side of the mid-continental highlands eons before the wagons bearing the children of Mattox Mays ever rattled down it, and before the time of man on earth.

In the beginning, a great rumpling of the earth's rock mantle pushed up the Appalachians and Blue Ridge Mountains, and left the crease in the blanket of earth between these ranges known as the Valley of Virginia. The springtide rushes of meltwater, seeking the sea, found the valley, and engraved their streambeds and rivers into it. The green came, then the animals; and thousands of years before any human foot fell on that terrain, the buffalo found in the long margins of the valley's waters pleasant routes to their open foraging grounds, shrinking as the vast forest darkness tracked northward behind the retreating ice sheets. Their hooves wore the trails that the first of our own kind, the aboriginal hunters on the American continents, paced south from the Great Lakes to trade or make war with other nations in what is now Virginia and the Carolinas.

The Europeans exploring inland in the seventeenth century found the trail, and called it the Warriors' Road. And after 1744, when aboriginal Americans treated away control of it to the British, it became known as the Great Philadelphia Wagon Road: for at Philadelphia it began, bending southward at the Potomac in Pennsylvania and thence south between the mountain ranges. The newcomers took to it first in a late winter trickle, then in a spring flood of thousands upon thousands—Germans and Englishmen hungry for the tracts of land opening up for their dominion in the pre-Revolutionary South, dissidents and missionaries and refugees belonging to myriad Protestant sects ousted from their European homelands, Indian traders from all the white tribes, and, most numerous and finally most influential of all, the Scots-Irish.

They came through the mountain passes in time to see what remained of eastern America's final primordial wilderness, and left written memoirs of what they saw. On November 24, 1752, the Moravian leader August Spangenberg, stopping on the corrugated and treacherous road south to what he called "Der Nord Carolina Land und Colonie Etablissement," noted in his diary: "The land is very rich, and has been much frequented by buffalo, whose tracks are everywhere, and can often be followed with profit. Frequently, however, a man cannot travel them, for they go through thick and thin, through morass and deep water, and up and down banks so steep that a man could fall down but neither ride nor walk." He reports hearing from the "pathless forest" the footfall of panthers, and the morning songs of wolves—tamer ones, he believes, than the ones he had known in the woods of central Europe. And he writes of the stubborn resistance of the flood-softened valley road to the transit of his companions, and to any smoothing by feet and wheels of travelers. Writing after his band of pilgrims had occupied their Carolina land, Spangenberg reports his fear of the Catawba and Cherokee who had once owned the trail; and many others who came that way, clearing pasturage and farmland on its waysides, have left their own records of the want and injury that dogged all the earliest travelers on the road south from Pennsylvania.

Only twenty years later, when William Hill and Dorcas and the children took to the road, the animals that had alarmed Spangenberg were retreating into the forests, or disappearing altogether. The roadside wilderness, from Virginia to the trail's end in the fur-trading settlement at Augusta, had been hacked back for livestock and plantations of apple and peach trees, tobacco and grain and turnips and pumpkins. My kin and ancestors did not go the whole distance to the road's end, at the edge of the Georgia colony. Instead they turned west just past the Blue Ridge Mountains, toward their promised land grants in sparsely populated woods and small, crumpled hills, lying between the Saluda and Savannah rivers in upper South Carolina.

They had come from a strange land; they arrived in a stranger one. As early as 1753, officials were returning from the upcountry to the old colonial headquarters at Charleston with news of a fracturing and breakdown of English civilization. It was unlike anything known to them, and unlike anything my own people had witnessed even along the Roanoke in late colonial Virginia. The new settlers "lived like Savages," Governor James Glen discovered—"ignorant, lazy, poor and . . . hardly able to exist in a harsh and sometimes hostile land," rearing their offspring with no more care than they would expend on "a litter of Piggs," and allowing them to grow up "equally naked and full as Nasty." Lawlessness prevailed, courts and legislative assemblies were nonexistent, venereal disease was nearly universal, legal marriage rare. And Glen was astonished to find a man who had seen neither church nor minister, no ship or "great Gun." A few years later, on the eve of my ancestors' journey down the Great Wagon Road, another colonial official found the denominations of reformed Christendom "subdivided ad infinitum in the back parts, as illiterate enthusiasm or wild imagination can misinterpret the Scripture"; and "every circle of Christian knowledge [growing] fainter as more removed from the center."

Such reports multiplied in number in the years immediately preceding the Revolution. Much of this official horror, surely, can be written down to the utter unfamiliarity of Charleston's cultivated Anglican elite with the radically *different* conditions prevailing on their colony's—any colony's—moving edge. But at least one contemporary observer, the Church of England cleric Charles Woodmason, laid the blame for these conditions at the doorstep of his fellow Charlestonians. "I must freely say, that it has been owing to the Inattention and Indolence of the Clergy, that the Sectaries have gain'd so much Ground here. While they [sat down] Easy and Quiet, enjoying the Delicacies of Life, they thought no more of the Church, or of her Interests than of the Empire of Japan." He calls the coastal elite "overgrown Planters who wallow in Luxury, Ease, and Plenty," and he derides their hypocrisy: "Lo! such are the Men who bounce, and make such Noise about Liberty! Liberty! . . . And at the same time keep half their Subjects in a State of Slavery."

But, in fairness to them, the shocked travelers from the low country to the frontier were ordinary English colonists, with the conservative ideas of civilization born of the oligarchic, authoritarian version of Enlightenment we have already seen flourishing in tidewater Virginia. Finding the largely Scots-Irish colonists untouched by any such vision of Augustan order, and hostile to it, the Charlestonians were as much dismayed as repulsed. For, to the endless frustration of well-meaning believers in the traditional Anglican culture deeply rooted on the Southern Atlantic seaboard, royal America was slipping out of their grasp. Another way of being on the land, charged with pioneering spirit, and can-do individualism, was being learned and established up the rivers from Charleston.

Like most Southerners of my generation—what the children of my countrymen learn in high-school civics classes today, I do not know—I was reared on the meat of Frontier mythology. Even when protesting U.S. involvement in Vietnam—when old textbook America First patriotism lay, for us, on the trash heap—I never seriously doubted that our demonstrations were rooted in a defense of the sturdy, peculiar freedom of distant people—freedom like that born in the nation's beautiful morning land of Conestoga wagons, raccoon hats, and muzzle-loading rifles, which we called the Frontier. Thereafter, for many years, I gave no thought to the sources of these ideas—until they returned to mind as I began trying to envision upper South Carolina at the time my ancestors arrived there, and witnessed again the three-way collision of Southern mythology, the evidence, and myself.

The evidence of this madness on the frontier is abundant—if biased, because written, for the most part, by bureaucrats and colonial officials and other true King's men, such as Charles Woodmason. Surely, Woodmason's tirades against the Scots-Irish Presbyterians, New Light Baptists, and other Christian sectarians of the backwoods—"Rhapsodists—Enthusiasts—Bigots—Pedantic, illiterate, impudent Hypocrites"—often grate on the ear with the metallic screech of ax-grinding. But even when we factor out the skew put into Woodmason's inner eyesight by his early life among England's gentry and his New World careers as planter, high public official, and Anglican priest, his journal and memoranda of upcountry travels in the late 1760s remain believable, and shed strong light on the landscape into which Dorcas Hill brought her Mays offspring.

If appalled, Woodmason was also honest. And, when not being merely another English snob and boor abroad, he was trying to conform his life as an Anglican priest in South Carolina to the worthy model provided by George Herbert, and a host of other seventeenth-century rural English clergy, for whom the greater part of true religion was meeting the everyday, practical needs of the people, high and ordinary. It meant caring about the education as well as the morality of his people, their methods of farming and the condition of roads and bridges, and all else that belongs to common life. He conducted himself accordingly when serving Christians in the civilized tidewater; and it was apparently with a good heart and genuine love for the isolated Anglican congregations planted far back of the tidewater that Woodmason first headed inland in 1766.

What this itinerant minister found was the same raw absence of orderly life, and the same civil anarchy and religious extremism, that had alarmed earlier official visitors. Some of the incidents Woodmason relates are funny—to us, if not to him—with an impudent, cranky humor that any Southerner will recognize at once as Southern indeed. Arriving in a makeshift meeting house to preach, for instance, the erstwhile clergyman finds a gang of Presbyterian toughs waiting for him, "who brought with them 57 Dogs (for I counted them) which in Time of service they set fighting"—and which, predictably, put a quick enough end to the sermon. In the same place, a man egged on by his co-religionists—hostile Baptists this time— steals Woodmason's nightgown from his room, "putting it on—then visiting a Woman in Bed, and getting to Bed to her, and making her give out next day, that the Parson came to Bed to her." (They apparently did not know, as the editor of Woodmason's papers tells us, that the unfortunate parson had been rendered impotent some time before by a kick from a horse.)

But the practical jokes Woodmason endured with little patience and much exasperation were played out against a background of seething sectarian turmoil, spreading along the shadowy creek bottoms of the upcountry like a fever. "These Sects are eternally jarring among themselves," he notes. "The Presbyterians hate the Baptists far more than they do the Episcopalians, and so of the Rest—But (as in England) they will unite altogether—in a Body to distress or injure the Church establish'd."

In the Anglican priest's narratives of the wars between rural Baptists and Presbyterians and other sects, and among themselves, we catch undeniably true glimpses of the upcountry backdrop against which my ancestor, Abney Mays, his brothers and sisters, came of age after the American Revolution. If what he witnessed is occasionally amusing, it is not always, and frequently horrifies. Perhaps believing him to be a missionary for some unwelcome sect, for example, a band of zealots—their leader later hanged, the rest banished—fall upon a traveler, "cut Him into Atoms singing Hymns, making Processions and Prayers, and offering up this inhuman Sacrifice to the Deity, as an acceptable Oblation." In another anecdote, we learn of a Church of Scotland minister for whom Woodmason had high regard—the Anglican priest's problem, after all, had less to do with Christian difference than the violence it has so often precipitated—who persisted in using the Lord's Prayer in private family devotions, after his backwoods congregation had banished it from public worship, and was murdered by his fellow Christians for it. Instances of extreme fanaticism such as these, however, are only the most egregious examples of social ruin in Woodmason's catalogue of more general destitution and terrible poverty, ignorance, ruin of roads and dwellings, neglect of children.

Imagining he, or the colonial elite, could ever have created Dorset in Carolina was foolish, if forgivable. The English and Anglican path of existence that had been the *first* culture of the South—infused with a belief in the rule of law and a code of life grounded in the Book of Common Prayer and English decency—was enjoying its last hour on the coastal plain between Williamsburg and Savannah, and quickly eroding even there. In the hills, the South's *second* culture, of anarchy and violence and bigotry, had already been conceived and brought forth, and sturdily come into its own. It has endured in Southern civilization, as the demon brother of whatever goodness our history on Southern land has bequeathed us, in the bizarre rites and malice of the Ku Klux Klan, in the lynchings officially condemned but tacitly condoned by the white Southern elite after the Civil War, in the murder of apostles of human rights during the 1960s. The blood of the victims, black and white and aboriginal, cries out from the ground, reminding modern Southerners that *this, too,* is what we are.

I have passed along the Carolina stretches of the Great Philadelphia Wagon Road in every season, scouting the rocky hollows and coves and steep forests along it. These wanderings began in the early 1960s, when I was an undergraduate at Bob Jones University, the famously Fundamentalist college in Greenville, South Carolina, not far from the North Carolina border. I went to Bob Jones, and stayed there, for the wrong reasons: not for its religion, its reason to exist, in which I never felt at home, but for its rigid authoritarianism. Looking backward to those days, I see a young man tormented by centrifugal forces, ill from a lifetime of repressing all desires, even the desire to exist, and who sought and found in this peculiar institution a welcoming culture of restriction and repression. In some deep place inside me, I already knew that such confinement could not restore the courage to exist I was losing. Unlike some other graduates I've run into over the years since leaving the place, however, I harbor no resentment toward Bob Jones, and have many good memories of the literary education and friendships I enjoyed there—especially the excellent introductions to the Southern writing and the Classical languages and literatures that cast deep roots into my thinking.

It was during those years that I took to making long drives outside Greenville every chance I got, into the beautiful countryside of upper South Carolina and into the Blue Ridge foothills. Eventually, I found a favorite destination: a tall, stony hill north of the city, on the border of North Carolina, that was sacred in its beauty, in its *otherness* to the world. I sought its tangled green solitudes often, to try thinking loose the knots that tightly bound me in my early twenties, trying to recall the South as it had been and was, what I was within it, and what our culture was inside me.

In those recollections on the mountain, I found myself trapped in a crevice between past and future, and among fluid contradictions given voice by the South's great modern novelists and storytellers of the years between world wars. They had written their conflicted annals on a fault line between tectonic plates of an agrarian, rural world shifting away into the irrevocable *past*, and of a huge, brightly tumultuous continent of *Americanism* grinding over the place where the South had once been. By the time I sought and found my thinking place on the Carolina mountain, the South was merely a certain stretch along the transcontinental Sun Belt, with an orange and aqua Howard Johnson's restaurant at every important interchange on the new interstate highway system, with whatever nurturing tales lying buried under pavement and forgetfulness. Yet since Faulkner the past had come to seem only more unrecoverable, the present more intolerable, the future, at least for me, unimaginable as a place of authentic dwelling.

I had come of age too late for the South, and too early for America—certainly too far along in time to believe freely and openly that the South of open fields, Classical learning, and sober tradition could be resurrected in fact. It was while transfixed in that interval, reading our Southern writers, that I found poets who had experienced this same entrapment in a world become unrecognizable.

I first encountered the poet Allen Tate's elegiac "Aeneas at Washington" in a course at Bob Jones, then often took it with me to the mountain: for it spoke what I could not speak, in words that I did not have. Tate's Aeneas, exile and legendary founder of Roman civilization, stands "in the rain, far from home at nightfall,"

By the Potomac, the great Dome lit the water,
The city my blood had built I knew no more
While the screech-owl whistled his new delight
Consecutively dark.

Stuck in the wet mire
Four thousand leagues from the ninth buried city
I thought of Troy, what we had built her for.

But what good could there be in meditating on a lost, ancient realm of virtue, buried four thousand leagues in the past, irretrievable? In another beautiful poem, "Ode to the Confederate Dead," Tate cries the same question:

What shall we say who have knowledge
Carried to the heart? Shall we take the act
To the grave? Shall we, more hopeful, set up the grave
In the house? The ravenous grave?

Never in America, in the shadow of that "great Dome" on the Potomac, but only in some restitution of the agrarian South's profound virtues, I imagined—Tate imagined—could there be any resolution to the heart's strife. Yet he admonishes:

Leave now
The shut gate and the decomposing wall:
The gentle serpent, green in the mulberry bush,
Riots with his tongue through the hush—
Sentinel to the grave who counts us all!

I could not abide Tate's warning to "leave now" the past—for, hidden behind the "shut gate and decomposing wall" was, or seemed to be, the old Southern certainties I longed for. It was then, as I recall, that I began to construct in my mind a vision of those certainties, from selective memories of my father's plantation, the roads and sky, the house of my grandparents, with its familiar simplicities and order. Once this antiquated and unreal interior homeland was built, and the America I dreaded had receded—I spent many hours on my Carolina mountain, my thinking place, working on this fantastical architecture in my head—it became easy to forget the more complex realities present from the beginning with my selectively remembered tatters.

I did *not* remember the hard work of my grandfather John Matthew Mays, politician and rural industrialist, to bring New South modernity to his rural back-pocket of Louisiana. Or his successful campaigns in the 1920s to link his little town by good roads to the whirlwind of American mobility. The South's old feudalism was gradually being laid to rest behind "the shut gate and the decomposing wall" by the South's integration into centralized New Deal American liberalism. The last hurrahs for a possible Southern *distance* from America, and those who shouted them, were disappearing from life and relevance in J. M. Mays's South, in the 1920s and 1930s, along with whatever remained of agrarian idealism.

So it was that, afraid of assimilation, *contamination* by America, I retreated into a disorderly study of Southern literary witnesses to the turning point—my secret reason for visiting Oxford the first time—and later retreated into yet more remote fiefdoms of the mind, the languages and literatures of medieval Europe. And an anachronism I remained, a brittle, creaking self-construction denying half of what I was—until I could bear the contradictions of this exile into unreality no longer, and finally let the shadowy, haunted house I had become fall into the blinding, saving darkness of mental breakdown.

One of the first of those "thinking places" I ever found was located on the little hummock back of my childhood house at Spring Ridge. During my teenage years, as the families of my dead parents warred over my salvation—whether it would be on the path of my father's Methodism or that of my mother's Christian Science—I found peace beside a slow creek in the wooded hills north of Greenwood. Later, I found a place under a bridge in a park laid out by Frederick Law Olmsted in Rochester, New York. And I continued to find these thinking places, and have one now, decidedly less picturesque than Olmsted's park, in a marshy, weedy Toronto wasteland dotted by ruins of industrial emplacements.

But of them all, the mountain in South Carolina has remained the refuge I loved best, and wished to keep in memory as it was. That was not to be. After leaving the South, I did revisit the vicinity twice. The first occasion was nearly thirty years ago, in the company of an old Bob Jones friend then doing graduate English studies at the University of Tennessee. I was reluctant to go back, for two reasons. One was the prospect of finding it *parked*—tidied and well-roaded, and thick with the signage and regulations that have come with the transformation of enormous tracts of our Southern and wildwoods into tourist attractions. Another was the probability that the bright squalor of malls, franchises, and subdivisions had sprawled from the town near the hill. As it happened, the first of these fears was not justified; the second was justified richly. I resolved never to return to the place.

In the time of writing this book, however, I drove back to the mountain again. It was during a stay in a motel near Greenwood, South Carolina, which lies in the hills south of Greenville on which my ancestors and nearest kin lived between the 1770s and the Civil War.

Like most writers, perhaps, I am always writing something, *any-thing*, even when on the road—or especially then. So upon checking into yet another motel on the way, I pulled out my laptop and began to record the events of the day. What wanted to be written up was the beauty of the North Carolina mountains and South Carolina piedmont I'd come back to that spring—the deep green slopes lit from beneath the shade by the incandescent blossoms of mountain laurel and dogwood, the calming plash and tumble of water descending through the impenetrably wooded ravines, or along the slower courses. But having approached my old mountain that day for the first time in almost three decades, and witnessed the crawl up to it of even more ugliness than I'd witnessed when David and I were there, I found myself hating the South, and writing out that hatred against the Southerners who had allowed, or made, such ugliness come to pass.

I should have known better. The decay of the plantation houses and broad, quiet lands that had once taught me the Southern understanding of stable grace, the violation of the once-spacious lawn of a small-town mansion by a hideous gas station, a shabby modern apartment block crowding a once-elegant courthouse—such sights, and the creep of fast-food outlets and malls and wretched motels over all the upcountry landscape in which my own blood kin lay buried sickened me in ways a thousand hours spent in the South's declining beauty, or another twenty-five years of psychotherapy, or more barrels of psychoactive drugs, would never alleviate.

In another place, or in some more sober frame of mind, I would have recalled the public, economic reasons these desolations had occurred in this century. There was the Great Depression, which had visited misery and poverty on all the rural South; and the post-Depression emptying of the poverty-stricken countryside by the pull of cities hungry for industrial and service workers. In the small towns, elderly Southern matrons plunged into poverty, yet still wishing to live and die in the ample houses of their husbands and fathers, were forced to sell off rose gardens for transformation into trailer courts or horrible little malls. The long open roll of fields, through which the narrow roads ran up to the edge of town, became bordered with cheap enterprises that began to decay the day they were completed.

But the resentful disappointment I felt in that hour narrows the mind and imagination; and it was crippling what powers I possessed to penetrate the deteriorating façades and neglect lining the highways in that district, and to see the historical tragedy lying just beyond. For if Southerners have always admired graceful Classical architecture and built ample houses, and raised fine monuments to the dead, we have never cared much for, and often resisted, urban planning and land-use restrictions and the other instruments for keeping civic beauty intact. That neglect may once have been benign; but it now seemed to me malignant—a kind of forceful forgetting that carries in it the power to obliterate what is forgotten. In the end, I discovered, in that homely motel room, nothing could be written; so I went to bed, determined to think my way out of these oddly startling revulsions the next morning, or to leave.

The motel room did not qualify as a thinking place. But I knew of a spot, not far away, that might serve. It was a cemetery near the village of Hodges and the Cokesbury crossroads, where the remains of some of my earliest Carolina ancestors had lain since the early nineteenth century. I had found it on only one map, in a plain little booklet that happened to be for sale when I'd stopped, not long before, at the tourist center of the old Revolutionary battleground near the town of Ninety Six, close to where I was staying. Without it, I might never have known where to find the graveyard, or even that it existed.

The small treasury of inscriptions was completed in 1972 by the Watson sisters, Margaret and Louise, two in the legion of uncelebrated angel-guardians of local memory throughout the South, without whom anybody's search for roots deeper than yesterday would be impossible. The Watson sisters had drawn their findings, and their inspiration, from earlier researchers. One, their father Harry Watson, born in 1876, had been a newspaper editor. The other, Thomas C. Anderson, was his slightly older friend, and a planter and surveyor. Between them, these enthusiasts of local story and topography knew the district along the west side of the Saluda well, and kept notes on what they considered notable sites. Their notations, in turn, guided Watson's daughters to the 108 family cemeteries and the gravestone inscriptions recorded in the book I found.

In the years they were beating their way along overgrown tracks to forgotten graveyards, their effort was almost too late. Earlier clearers of family plots had stripped out much *Vinca minor,* the small-leafed periwinkle—a favorite old cemetery botanical, and, incidentally, an excellent antidote to erosion and overgrowth—perhaps because of periwinkle's ancient associations with death, even witchcraft. Meanwhile, large topographical changes had proved deadlier threats to memory than the removal of ground cover. "Roads, buildings and other points of reference have changed considerably since [Harry] Watson made his first notes," the sisters write in the introduction to their work. "What was once a forest is now a residential subdivision and a former pasture has become a forest in nearly 70 years. New roads have been cut and old ones abandoned, houses torn down or burned." But, for the sisters—and for all who push through the thickets of genealogical forgetfulness—the "death of many who knew so much but did not write it down is, of course, the greatest loss."

Even with the Watsons' fastidiously drawn map, it is not easy to find Walnut Grove Cemetery on its narrow rural road north of Hodges. The wayside burying ground beside Mulberry Creek, along which some of Mattox Mays's children scattered to begin their farms, is now obscured by a screen of brush, and dark in a thicket of tall hardwood trees festooned with wrist-thick vines. The first time by, I missed it, and had to check the map again; the second time, a white tooth of marble shining in the brush caught my eye. And wading through the weeds and thickets near the stone, I soon found the plots where lie the bones of my ancestor Matthew Mays (1790–1842), grandchild of Mattox and Dorcas, and his wife, Lucretia Rogers (1797–1845). And nearby lie those of my great-great-grandfather Meade Mays, born in 1818 and dead, a young man, in early 1849. Meade's grave is under a stone bearing a text with the stale air of carver's doggerel about it, but with a hint at circumstances an embittered widow might want glancingly commemorated:

Rest[s] here his heart
upon the lap of earth
'Tis Wisdom's reproof
to those who enjoy mirth.

A short time before my arrival at Walnut Grove, someone—a cousin perhaps, whom I may never meet, whose name I may never know—had come here, and put fresh roses beside the well-carved and inscribed monument marking the grave of Matthew Mays.

As a rule, I do not find the graveyards of my ancestors and relations melancholy. If Walnut Grove was dusky with a certain unfamiliar sadness, long neglect had made it so. In 1826 a place of assembly for local Christians—Baptists for the most part, but probably also Presbyterians and perhaps Methodists—had been built on this land sloping down to Mulberry Creek. Burials in the adjacent cemetery had begun by 1828. But in the high summer of 1850, not many months after the bones of Meade Mays were put down into Walnut Grove, the farms along the creek were subjected to a hot spell that threatened the farms, hence the people, with ruination. "Prayer for rain was made at the meeting house," a recent chronicler of Walnut Grove Baptist Church has written, "and it came when an all day meeting was being held in July. As the heavy rain caused the creek to overflow the low area, men unhitched their horses, and all persons crowded into the buildings. When the electric storm became very bad, the women removed the steel hoops in their skirts and piled them in the middle of the church and then became still more frightened." Saddles were swept away from under the church by the floodwaters of Mulberry Creek, and the mules and horses fled to higher ground. And so did the Christians, shortly after the Lord had answered their prayer *too* abundantly. The new meeting place and cemetery were established on a hill a mile or so away, and the assembly abandoned the bodies of their earlier communicants to the wild green that quickly engulfs any patch of cleared Southern ground left untended.

The cemetery they left behind will probably not remain isolated under its canopy of shade trees for long. Already, the bungalows and businesses and other vanguards of suburban sprawl—the various incarnations of ugliness that had brought me to this thinking place— are spreading along a busy nearby highway, covering what once were pastures and the edges of old plantations. For now, however, our long Southern springs and summers continue to mantle the site with thickets for birds and rabbits, gradually and quietly absorbing my ancestors' graves into Southern forest. There are few people who recall where these long-dead kinsmen lie. Eventually no one will remain to remember. Is that so terrible a thing or thought? I do not know where old William Mays, priest and primordial American ancestor, is buried; or John Maies, or Mattox, or myriad other Mays relations. Before Aunt Vandalia died, and I set out on these journeys though the Southern mind and land, such ignorance did not bother me. Almost all my kin and ancestors, after all, were ordinary people, of the sort who are born into the world, live awhile, doing nothing grand, and die, then pass gradually into the forgetfulness that allows the living to think their own thoughts, unhaunted by ancestral voices.

But try as I might that day, I could not rid myself of a certain grief at the impending disappearance of the graves by Mulberry Creek into nothingness, if only because their last concealment will almost certainly not be gradual, or kindly. The cemetery long ago passed from the ownership and oversight of Walnut Grove Baptist Church into other hands. And with only a few scattered descendants to remember it, and no one, so far as I know, inclined to spare it, the burying ground now lay exposed to a force infinitely more destructive than weather and woods. It was the same aggressive forgetfulness churning in Southern culture that appalled me about the squalid gas station squatting on the graceful mansion's front yard, the same contempt toward so many ordinary monuments and architectures—whether or not they have anything to do with my ancestors is almost irrelevant—that remain to remind contemporary Southerners of our long dwelling on the land, the obligation we bear to remember its beauties.

That day in the graveyard was largely spent in thinking about memory, remembering and forgetting—so perhaps it was not as odd as it now seems that, while walking the uneven ground under which my kin lay, I was unexpectedly reminded of a man I'd met not long before, whose relationship with memory was the strangest I'd ever heard of. His name was William Thompson, and the place we met was Dr. Oliver Sacks's remarkable collection of neurological case histories called *The Man Who Mistook His Wife for a Hat*. The disorder from which William suffered is known as Korsakov's syndrome, which condemns its victims to an inability to hold anything in memory for more than an instant. "Abysses of amnesia continually opened beneath him," writes Sacks, "but he would bridge them, nimbly, by fluent confabulations and fictions of all kinds." They were not, however, fictions to *his* mind, but the elements of a "wholly normal, stable and factual world. So far as *he* was concerned, there was nothing the matter."

For Dr. Sacks, the pathos of William's derangement lay in his patient's condemnation to cobbling together incessantly a fantastical world for himself—a simulation of the unique story by which each of us recognizes himself, communicates himself—from the scraps and tatters of language whirling in his brain. We must have such stories, or perish; unwilling to perish, William invented a story of himself each moment. Sacks comments: "This narrative need, perhaps, is the clue to Mr. Thompson's desperate tale-telling, his verbosity. Deprived of continuity, of a quiet, continuous, inner narrative, he is driven to a sort of narrational frenzy—hence his ceaseless tales, his confabulations, his mythomania. Unable to maintain a genuine narrative . . .

he is driven to the proliferation of pseudo-narratives, in a pseudo-continuity, pseudo-worlds peopled by pseudo-people, phantoms."

The mind of the South is not that of William Thompson. But the course of Southern history, it seemed to me, was an instance of something eerily similar to this neurological condition, spread out over the long rhythms of time and generalized through our regional culture. The lawlessness and apocalyptic hysteria Charles Woodmason and many others witnessed on the frontier, the Revolution's violent, ideological rejection of our European civilization, the malling and paving of the Southern land, correspond to the disastrous erasures of memory in the Korsakov symptomatology—even as the endless storytelling of Southerners, our cherished myths of the "Colonial," or the "Frontier," the embalming of certain architectures, attitudes, political views in the formaldehyde of "Old South" myth, display the mixed oddity and familiarity that we find in William's made-up histories.

The analogy that occurred to me in the graveyard by Mulberry Creek could be pressed no further without risking absurdity. Still, memory—or, more accurately, *how* to remember, to receive, the words of our ancestors—is a problem at the heart of Southern culture. In my college days at Bob Jones University, I had opened myself to possession by these Southern voices, which almost drowned out my own. In Rochester, during the healing ordeal of psychotherapy, I had recovered my voice and soul, and thereafter would try hard not to attend too closely to the whispers from Southern land and memory. But more recently I had learned, in an old Episcopal church on Chesapeake Bay and by the waters of the Appomattox and Staunton, that I could listen, and not be possessed; and that such listening is the necessary first step toward an honoring of the past, and of the Southern blood and family to which I belong. Shuffling in the sediment of wet leaves and fallen branches on Walnut Grove cemetery's unfenced grounds, I was grateful to have seen the monuments of my forebears unhidden, still witnessing to those who worked in this place, died, and became one with the Southern earth, the old nurse of our own lives and dreams.

Coming of age in the decades following the Revolution, the Mays children of Dorcas Abney Hill acquired their own substantial lands

along the west side of the Saluda River and its tributaries, such as
Mulberry Creek, and founded their own plantations. The cessation of
Revolutionary war in the 1780s throughout newly republican South
Carolina did not inaugurate the Golden Age prophesied by the more
radical ideologues of revolt; my ancestors and kin born before 1776
continued to live *mutatis mutandi* as they had in Virginia, before that
momentous date—raising crops of tobacco, hemp, wheat, and meat,
sending them downriver to the republic's eastern seaboard markets,
buying and swapping land, and enriching themselves, as their own
Mays ancestors had done in America for almost two centuries. The
rhythm of Southern seasons and weathers did not change; so neither
did my family's practice of upcountry living and farming change
much until well into the nineteenth century.

What did change after the Revolution was the spiritual atmo-
sphere in which my kinsmen lived. The social and religious turmoil,
the anarchy and conflict witnessed by Charles Woodmason subsided
as the new century approached; courts and justice were introduced,
the traditions of English common law were restored, and a sense of
order prevailed for the first time among the people of the hills.
Anglicanism, at least as represented by the new American Episcopal
Church, did not recover its hold on the imagination of my family,
now largely Methodist. But the old traditions of Anglican piety, disci-
pline, and moral seriousness, revived and preached by the priest
John Wesley, did so.

At first, due to the isolation of the farms along the Saluda, my
Methodist ancestors worshipped in a common house of prayer with
Baptists and Calvinists, receiving the sacraments of Baptism and Holy
Communion from whatever itinerant minister happened to be avail-
able. And they accepted burial in whatever holy ground lay
nearby—in the case of several relations, the cemetery of Baptists on
Mulberry Creek. What counts in all this is the renewed spirit of religious tolerance, and renewed respect for the institutions of government and justice and learning, much of it pioneered by Methodist
missionaries and local layfolk. But equally important is the *tenor* of
this Saluda Methodism. Its finest surviving witness is surely the
Cokesbury Conference School building, eight miles outside Greenwood. The structure now standing is a tall, severe Classical temple
elevated (like a Palladian mansion) by a pedestal one story high, and

was put up in 1855 to replace an earlier edifice. As recent as it is, the school is also stiffly *archaic*, as though built to recall the contents of the education propounded on its beautiful hilltop site for decades before 1855: as heavy on Classical morality and Stoic virtue as on Wesleyan piety.

The architectural style of the building was created within the psychological absence that everywhere followed the American Revolution, as the most thoughtful citizens in the new confederation of states found themselves independent, but without a culture that could be called distinctly *American*. If this absence did not bother many farmers in the early republic, it did prompt an extraordinary hunger for an American Revolutionary chic among the merchants, great Eastern industrialists, and other captains of social opinion. So it was, with the quixotic verve of early republican culture, that they borrowed wholesale from the rejected British monarchy the first republican national architectural and decorative manner; and began to build.

The choice fell on the over-refined, deliberately archaeological style known, in America, as *Federal*—the only decorative style in history, to my knowledge, named after a political faction. It was the most widespread republican strategy of decor and building by the end of the 1780s, when the more advanced cultural centers began to be adorned with much elegant curving and swagging, and spindly columns—all in an attempt to give the Classical models of the colonial period a self-consciously unselfconscious *ancient* look. If the artificiality of this styling was always at loggerheads with more radical advocates of antique simplicity, of the sort championed by Patrick Henry, the partisans of the Federal, both party and style, promoted still other contradictions. For the Federal was meant to serve as a vehicle for declaring an *American* refinement, while turning out to be an entirely *English* refinement; it was a visual rhetoric meant surely to argue for freedom, though the freedom of an *English nobleman* of the Georgian period—the gracious, liberal ease that can only be sustained by wealth, property, privilege, and a toiling underclass held in servitude.

Such contradictions eventually absorbed the omnivorous attention of Thomas Jefferson, who opposed the antiquarian Federal style on ideological grounds, and promoted a plainer version of architectural Classicism, which would become important in the South's construction of its regional identity before the Civil War. But not yet. In the decades on either side of 1800, the Federal style was the *American* style, North and South, informing decor and detail and frame everywhere along the urban Atlantic edge of America, from Boston to the northern edge of Florida. Among the manner's early masterpieces, and perhaps the most familiar to all Americans, is George Washington's Mount Vernon, from the 1780s—but despite this and other exemplary works, the Federal style in architecture never captivated Southern imagination. The Federal style of *thinking*, however—autocratic and militant in bearing, ultimately imperial Roman in inspiration—did scatter throughout the South during the post-Revolutionary settlement of allegiances and ideals, taking root nowhere among my early republican kinsman more firmly than in the quick, ready mind of Samuel Mays.

Among the children of Dorcas and Mattox Mays, Samuel was different. In matters of economy, his two brothers Abney (my ancestor) and William were content to replicate their father's pacific Virginia path on Carolina ground, garnering enough land and slaves to become well-settled planters, and remaining otherwise free of ambition to own or become anything more. Had the War of Independence cast many sparks into their upper South Carolina districts, young William and Abney might have joined the local militia and fought; it did not, and these two sons apparently made no effort to seek military adventure during the epoch of revolt.

But Samuel, not yet twenty, went off to war with the republican militia no later than 1780, when British troops invaded South Carolina, and he fought in three battles that year. From time to time, throughout a long career as a planter and politician, he put on his uniform to serve the republic's military needs—from 1794 to 1814 as lieutenant colonel of a South Carolina regiment, and, from 1814 to 1816 as brigadier general of the state's First Brigade. And again unlike his brothers, when still in his twenties Samuel set about acquiring, by grant and purchase, very large estates along the Saluda and involving himself in the affairs of his state as a highly active, influential member of the legislative assembly from 1796 to 1805, and a senator from 1806 to 1813. At the time of his death, in 1816, Samuel Mays left his heirs and beneficiaries a great fortune that included some five thousand acres of farmland, seventy-eight slaves, and a wealth of tools, cotton, horses, and other possessions. Such is the historical record of Samuel, who, incidentally, broke an unwritten law almost universally obeyed by us Mayses of the South, simply by *becoming* historical, and famous in his time.

Composing a genealogical memoir in his Florida orange grove during the late 1920s, Samuel Edward Mays wrote in awe of his great-grandfather's military deeds and civil possessions, garlanding the documentary portrait with the laurels of family story. General Mays, according to Samuel Edward's account, was a man born to war, and destined to found a dynasty of warriors. He was also born to blood: the year after his three battles against the British, he lost a kinsman and his own grandfather, the parent of Dorcas Abney, in a legendary raid by the antirepublican Saluda terrorist "Bloody Bill" Cunningham. After the return of order in the 1780s, "[h]e was one of twenty men especially thanked by Congress for bravery; and for some especial act of bravery done by him and his brother Abney"— almost certainly acting as a civilian—"a commission was offered to Abney, who declined it, saying that it belonged to his younger brother Samuel. What became of the commission no one knows for [Samuel] died in 1816, and his sons, pioneering in Florida, were plunged into the Seminole Indian Wars." Samuel again went to war in 1812, when renewed hostilities broke out between Britain and her former American colonies. The old general ended his days, writes his great-grandson, in the cloud of empyrean glory to which he had aspired since boyhood—"a man of great prominence and wealth, having much personal acquaintance with great men of his day, including President Washington."

Notwithstanding his peculiarity among Dorcas's sons, I would probably not be writing about Samuel Mays were it not for a brief document that intrigued me from the time I found it: an inscription, said to have been discovered on a stone erected at Samuel's grave by the writer's father, Samuel Elias Mays, who died in 1906 in Florida. This old gentleman and Civil War veteran, at some unspecified date, had sought out "the old Mays Cemetery and copied the inscriptions. The place is about 15 miles southeast from Greenwood [S.C.], on the river where Gen. Mays owned a large plantation. A great many slaves were buried there. . . . The cemetery is not used any more and there are very large trees now growing up among the graves, over-turning the marble tombstones, some of which were broken." The complete text discovered on Samuel's tombstone, and reproduced in Samuel Edward's 1929 book, reads as follows:

> Sacred to the memory of General Samuel Mays who was born 23rd of July, 1762, and departed this unsullied life on the 25th of January, 1816. He was a man of frugal habits, of persever-ing industry, of incorruptible integrity. The events of his life formed an interesting commentary upon the formation of our free institutions. Without any advantages of birth or fortune, he acquired a reputable independence, and enjoyed for many years the honor of a seat as a member for this district in the seat of the Senate of this state.
>
> The born justice of his heart and the kindness of his man-ners deservedly endeared him to his surviving wife and chil-dren who have caused this monument to be erected.

At some time between the visit of Samuel Edward's father and the 1972 compilation by Margaret and Louise Watson, who repro-duce the epitaph in their book but could not find it, the inscribed stone was removed. Its present location is unknown. If everything *before* the prosaic third sentence—"The events of his life formed an interesting commentary upon the formation of our free institu-tions"—could have been written by someone in the early nineteenth century, all else sounds late, and probably is. In nearby cemeteries of the district, the simple, early grave markers were occasionally replaced by their descendants with grander stones bearing more ver-bose inscriptions, and I suspect this is what happened here. The stone's attribution to General Samuel's wife, Nancy Grigsby, is proba-bly honorary, and the whole composition may well have been the work of one of Samuel's distinguished offspring—Rhydon Mays, per-haps, a doctor and Florida orange planter—who had returned at an unknown date to pay proper tribute to his father.

Be all that as it may, the portrayal of Samuel Mays, who appears only in distant, bold outline against the horizon of South Carolina history, is perhaps loaded with more truth about this old warrior's self-understanding than his descendants may have realized. For

while Samuel was born "without any advantages of birth or fortune"
in pre-Revolutionary Virginia, the family portrait of him preserved in
the epitaph, and in Samuel Edward's 1929 book, is infused with the
cultural rhetoric of the early republic, dissolving the human visage
and replacing it with a certain contrived *type* of early American
face—Roman, militant, *Federal*, and, in this sense, *American, and not
yet Southern*. Samuel is surely not a Southerner of the sort who was
cobbled on antiquarian, romantic lasts in the slaveholding states
before the Civil War. Samuel is "kind," but not genteel. His recol-
lected virtues are the hard, Roman ones of industry and integrity and
justice. In the imagery of his will and the inscription and Mays family memory, he emerges as an ancient warrior at rest among riches
won in battles against human enemies or wrested from Nature. He is
also a successful businessman—no gently born rural aristocrat, or
heir to wealth he did not earn.

He is also pagan: for if fulsome funeral epitaphs and long passages
of pious and patriotic doggerel abound in the cemeteries of the district, virtually all those catalogued by the Watson sisters bear some
reference to Divinity, or heaven, or faith, or the gloom of death; and
Samuel's does not. He is presented as no exemplar of upcountry
Christian piety, but as the very incarnation of "frugal habits, of per-
severing industry, of incorruptible integrity"—the virtues we would
expect to find in someone who played the role of the Roman farmer
Cincinnatus in the military dramas of his time. Never mind that
Samuel stayed close to the center of contemporary political life
throughout his career, supervising his farms beyond the Saluda from
afar—unlike the fabled Roman military hero who left his plow, saved
the day, then returned to his farm beyond the Tiber. Coming of age
in a culture without historical precedents, he assumed the Roman
roles hallowed by American Revolutionary rhetoric: Cincinnatus,
when the situation called for it; and, during his long tenure in state
government, the eloquent and patriotic Cicero—the Enlightenment's
favorite Roman, whom Diderot hailed as a *"prodigy* of eloquence and
patriotism." (The elevation of Samuel in his descendants' collective
memory to the position of "founder" of South Carolina College at
Columbia, later the University of South Carolina—he was in fact
only a member of the state committee that established its charter—
may well spring from a half-thought wish to see him in the proxim-

ity of the gods and ancient worthies: for no educational institution in the antebellum South surpassed the college as an academy of Classical studies.)

That Samuel Mays played these literary, antique parts well seems probable; that he played them with all the faithfulness to the Enlightenment script he could muster is, to my mind, certain. The public men of the early years of the United States dwelt in a mental landscape populated by the Ancients. One did not have to don a mask from the wardrobe of Classical history to survive in the new America; the careers of Abney and William Mays show us that. Nor, were one's ambitions to lead and govern, was it enough merely to strike the pose of a Roman warrior, full of desirable virtues. Anyone aspiring to leadership and senatorial performance—at least in the Southern states at the beginning of the republic—needed most urgently the land Samuel made sure he owned in abundance. His holdings in the upcountry were far larger than anyone required for a decent living; but their vast extent was crucial to Samuel's hold on his chosen mask of life. As it did for Southern politicians before and long after the Civil War—as it did for the lawyer Lucius Quintus Cincinnatus Lamar, who disliked farming and rural life—the ownership of farmland gave to Samuel Mays the aura and authority of Augustan Americanism, without which he probably could never have achieved his public ambitions.

But Samuel, of course, did *not* stay clear of towns at any time in his adult life, as Jefferson urged all Americans to do, and spent most of his public life in one; and he probably never put his hand to a plow after he bolted out of William and Dorcas's door to war when barely eighteen. But, again, it hardly matters. He had the land, the key credential in his curriculum vitae, and the cachet that went with it—the land, his age's passport to the larger life young Samuel probably started to hanker after the day he hopped out of stepfather William's wagon onto South Carolina dirt for the very first time.

The disappearance of Samuel Mays's burying place in the nearly impenetrable commercial softwood forest now covering its Saluda River headland was far advanced by that spring morning when I went looking for it several years ago, and almost a century after Samuel Elias Mays had been there with his pencil and notepad.